2017 US
By Stan Mc

Comprehensive and unsurpassed

After 16 years, this coin guide remains unsurpassed in its ability to provide hundreds of coin errors as recognized by the world leading coin experts from ANA, PCGS, and NGC. Since 2000, this book has been the most comprehensive guide available with all known coin errors recognized by the major encapsulation services and sold by credible auction houses.

Searching for coins in circulation that contain errors can be a rewarding experience. Pocket change, bank rolled coin, and looking through old collections are some of the methods for error seekers. Numerous error coin photographs for coins that can still be located in circulation listed in the last chapter.

Most double die coins have very clear doubling with the bulk of the doubling in the date, the mintmark or the word "LIBERTY." On page 12 is an artist's depiction of true doubling verses machine doubling. The collector can use the drawing as a concise method of ensuring that the doubling is authentic.

Above is a sample of the doubling of a Lincoln cent. Detailed photographs shown in chapter 15 for coins that can be located in circulation today.

This edition includes errors struck on incorrect planchets. Error coins minted on planchets not intended for the minting of the coin are mules[1]. As evidenced by the numerous planchet errors bought and sold recently, the US Mint still creates many error coins with one denomination stamped on another.

The large number of error coins makes it impossible to photograph all types listed in this book. There is a distinct difference between a machine double coin and true double die coin. Our reference guide can validate the error and show the range of values as realized at auctions.

---

[1] Mules – Coins minted on planchets not intended for the particular mintage.

2

Table of Contents

Preface

This book provides the coin collector with a detailed description of the following:

- The minting process from US Mint sources
- A detailed description of mint error classifications with photographs.
- A comprehensive listing of all US error coins as cataloged by PCGS, ANACS, and NGC and sold at major auctions.
- An updated listing of all known error coins by coin, date, and auction sale price from high- end auction companies.

There are thousands error coins that have been encapsulated by PCGS, NGC, and ANACS. Many coin errors are very valuable while others sell for less than the cost the coin encapsulation.

Error coins can have a wide range of sales prices for the same dated coin with the same grade and error type. It is difficult to understand why a coin with the same date, error, and grade encapsulated by the same coin service can have a wide range of selling prices. This book presents a range of prices paid at auctions for each auctioned coin.

The findings of certified error coins sold at auction is the content of this book. In 2014, we started listing newly added coin errors with the year "20xx noted next to the find. We do not list raw coins not certified by PCGS[2], NCG[3], or ANACS[4] so that what we list is only authenticated error coins. We recognize that there are other coin encapsulation services; however, they are not as revered by collectors and we will not add any of these findings to this book.

It is very possible that one grading service can grade a coin lower or higher than another service. Experts in grading may at times take one coin graded by a service, and have it re-graded by another service with success of obtaining a higher grade. In some cases, this could be a difference of several thousand dollars.

---

[2] PCGS – A certification service of encapsulated coins. Professional Coin Grading Service.
[3] NGC – A certification service – Numismatic Guarantee Corporation.
[4] ANACS – An encapsulation coin service established in 1972. -American Numismatic Association

As an avid collector for 50 years, I have bought and sold thousands of US coins at auction. My interest in coins has led to the publication of a coin guide based upon completed auction results from major auction companies, live auctions, and coin shows. No other coin guide provides this information. This book has been selling on Amazon since 2000 with much success.

Over the years, I have seen thousands of coins that missed struck, and off center. Most of the finds have been minor in nature resulting in a low value for the type of error found. For the fortunate few that stumble across a true error, coin the reward can be very profitable. Error coin collecting has increased in popularity since the 1970's. Thousands of coins are in circulation and in private collections that go undiscovered with the types of errors described in this book. The evidence for coins that have circulated before the coin error discovery is with the coins that are graded in extra fine and lower conditions by the major encapsulation services. There are thousands of examples of error coins graded in good through extra fine condition and many of these coins are worth hundreds of dollars, if not thousands of dollars.

It takes a lot of patience to search through thousands of coins in order to pick out a coin that meets the standard classified as an error coin. Over the years, I searched though thousands coins seeking to find some of the elusive error coins such as the 1969-S double die Lincoln cent that can sell upwards of $20,000.

Chapter 1 – Classifications of Coin Varieties

There are three categories of error coins as provided by ANA[5]. Metal usage and striking errors refer widely as "planchet[6] errors", die errors, and mint striking errors. This does not include the varieties that the US Mint has issued over the years.

The modern day method of minting coins is to punch the coin stock in the size and configuration for stamping first. For cents, sheet stock in circular arrangement is used and then the surface and edge are prepared for minting. The blanks enter the dies for stamping and the obverse and reverse of the coin.

---

[5] ANA – American Numismatic Association
[6] Planchet – The raw blank that the mint uses to press the coin details.

Since the inception of coin collecting, there has been much controversy over what constitutes a true mint error.

We cannot emphasize enough the importance of obtaining a professional opinion concerning the type of error and the potential value of the error before sending it to an encapsulation service. If you believe, you have an error coin the best practice is to bring it to a coin dealer that is certified as an ANA and or PNG[7] dealer to obtain an opinion.

Planchet Errors

The word "planchet" is a term used by the US Mint and coin collectors for the blank and the blanks with upsets on the edge of the coin. A type I planchet is the blank itself. A type II planchet is the blank with the edging rolled on it. The type of planchet error is important in the classification of error coins and the value of the coins.

An improper alloy mixture constitutes a coin error. For example, a sheet of stock used for the minting of cents may have the incorrect proportion of copper and zinc in places that create some coins with uneven layers of the different metals. There are cases of Roosevelt dimes that are missing the nickel layer on the surface of the coin, thus a Roosevelt dime minted on a copper alloy planchet. In addition, there have been cases of Lincoln cents missing the copper surface revealing a coin minted on a zinc planchet.

Using the incorrect planchet in the minting process is another form of error. For example, a State Quarter minted using a Sacagawea dollar coin blank. The result is a State Quarter minted on an intended golden dollar blank. A coin minted on a planchet from a metal change such as a copper 1943 cent is a transitional error.

---

[7] PNG – Professional Numismatics Guild

Above is a Washington quarter struck on a dime planchet

Clipped Planchets

A planchet error also refers to many types of issues with obtaining a perfect blank for minting. Many of these planchet errors are missing portions of the edge of the coin or most of the planchet itself. The most common error is a planchet that results in a half moon. Coins missing part of the planchet are "clipped" planchets. Some of the planchet errors can be severe with various types of missing pieces of the coin and classified as curved clips, bowtie clips, assay clips etc. The most common clip is the curved clip as shown below:

1982-P Roosevelt Dime clipped planchet

Lamination Error
A dirty or oily blank may cause the details of the coin to become dull or even missing. A piece of debris may find its way into the dies causing a series of lines minted on the surface of the coin.

A lamination error results when the coin surface is peeling or cracking. Lamination errors are normally not of significant value; however, there are collectors that value these coins and they will pay a premium for unusual types of lamination issues.

Above is a 1943 Jefferson nickel with a lamination error

Planchet errors created from uneven stock makes the coin thicker or thinner than intended. The weight of the coin verses the normal intended weight contributes to the value of the coin. Thousands of Lincoln cents range in thickness from one end of the coin to the other. These are not of any significant value.

9

Mules

Mules are coins minted on planchets other than the designated one.

Above is a Washington quarter minted on a dollar planchet.

Die Errors

Die errors are those caused by the mint dies wearing down over time, broken dies, or dies that have not been prepared identical to the original replaced dies.

Dies that wear down over time may result in coin missing the finer details. Jefferson nickels minted before the 1990's, for example, have a tendency to be missing the lines in the steps on the reverse of the coin. Some early dated Jefferson nickels with full steps are valued in the thousands because of the rarity related to the poor minting process. Many collectors are only interested in the grade of a coin and not the specific details of full steps for a Jefferson nickel or full torch lines for a Roosevelt dime. The full torch designation began in the late 1990's by PCGS. Thousands of Roosevelt dimes exist in older holders that include the full torch designation. We have found that the full torch designation for Roosevelt dimes has not attracted much attention from the collecting community that would result in premiums paid for full torch Roosevelt dimes. The full line detail in the Franklin half liberty bell does have a major impact in the value of the coin, especially in the highest MS grades.

When the mint die suffers a fracture and this crack feature transposes onto the coins in the minting process. Coins minted with a die crack have a thin line or lines raised running across the surface of the coin. Below is a photograph show how a die crack results in a raised line on the surface of the coin. Note the horizontal lines running through the vines.

Die Cud

There are gouges in coins caused by flaws in dies, and die polishing mistakes resulting in coins minted with surface indentations, or polishing lines. A die cud occurs when part of the die breaks away and the metal flows into the break in the minting process. Below is a cud error on a Lincoln cent. Note the extra material near the left wheat stalk.

Die Cap

A "die cap" error has the appearance of a soda bottle cap with some of the details inside the cap. Coins stuck in the die and stamped several times are die cap errors.

Above-Die cap error 1999 Lincoln cent

Die Clash

A coin minted with traces of the reverse on the obverse or the opposite are "die clash" errors. Die clash errors result in the minting dies pressed together without a planchet between the dies. In subsequent stampings of planchets, the coins minted contain some of the reverse or obverse on opposite sides of the coin.

Found by the author in change, a 1970 Lincoln cent with the pillars stamped on the obverse. Value <$10.

Brockage

Brockage refers to a type of error coin in which one side of the coin has the normal design and the other side has a mirror image of the same design impressed upon it.

Above is a 1952 Washington quarter with brockage

Before 1990, all US coin dies were subject to mintmark errors resulting from the preparation of the dies. Hammering the mint- mark into the die manually sometimes causing a die to have a doubling. In the minting process, this would create a series of coins with a distinct of slight doubling of the mintmark. Hundreds of these errors can be located on the internet for sale noted as RPM's[8]. There are also RPD's[9] (re-punched dated coins); some of which are very valuable. RPD's have the date punched over the tops of the numbers of the raised date. These errors are not actual doubling of the date but raised lines are on the numbers indicating multiple dates struck over the original date.

A number of notable error coins exist with one mintmark on the die punched over another mintmark. The mint

---

[8] RPM – Re-punched mint mark
[9] RPD – re-punched date

14

intentionally used one die, in this case a San Francisco mint die and converted this die to a Denver mint die. These coins are over mintmark errors, or OMM.[10] One OMM Lincoln cent of note is the 1944-D over S mintage. The OMM noted as a DDO by the encapsulation services.

Some coins discovered with dates that appear multiple times in various locations on the coin are MPD's[11] (misplaced dates). MPD's are extremely rare and none located at the time of this book publication.

RPM's

A repunched mintmark is the result of a skilled mint worker hammering in a mintmark on the coin manually to repair it. Coin dies used before 1986 required rework to continue using them. When the mint worker hammered in the mintmark to rework it, sometimes the alignment was off creating a doubling or an RPM.

True double die coins result with a missed alignment of the die to hub. The hub is the master die.

Above is a typical RPM

Most mintmark doubling before 1986 is likely to be an RPM.

---

[10] OMM – Over mint mark
[11] MPD – Misplaced date

Double Dies

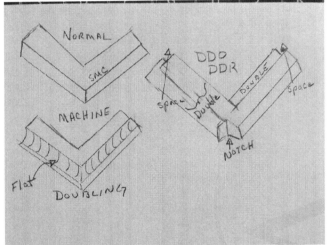

Above is the author's rendition of hub doubling and machine doubling on coins.

The normal lettering and dates shown above in the upper left. The machine doubling shown below and to the left reveals flat doubling. The drawing in the upper right shows notches and spaces with the doubling the same height as the normal letter and numbering.

The classification of a double die coin can be a very difficult task for those professionals that try to determine if a coin is a true double die or the result of the minting equipment that is not fine tuned casing a machine error. Defective hubs[12] are the root cause of doubling.

Collectors refer to double dies as DDO[13] - Double die obverse coins, DDR[14] – Double die reverse and OMM – Over mintmark.

Die creation as described by the US Mint on their web site www.USMINT.org is in detail below taken directly from the US mint site word for word. A good understanding minting process help the collector to understand how errors occur.

"The process of making working dies begins by creating a master hub. Making this master hub starts with a steel blank.

---

[12] Hub – the tool used to create a die. It is the mirror image of a die in reverse.
[13] DDO – Double die obverse
[14] DDR – Double die reverse

When the CNC milling machine cuts the coin design into the end of the steel blank, it creates a "master" hub. This process is repeated for a different design on a second hub representing the design for the opposite side of the coin. The master hub is then used to create a "master die." Dies start out as cylindrical steel blanks with a cone-shaped end. After machining, the die blank moves down a conveyor to the polishing machine.

A robot-like arm picks up the machined blank with a gripper that can load one blank into the polisher while unloading another. The polishing machine shines the cone end to a mirror-like finish.

Machinists measure the cone with a gauge before it continues to the inventory queue.

A working hub is formed.

Each working hub creates batches of dies that strike the final circulating coins.

Most U.S. coin production starts with the arrival of coils— rolled-up strips of flat metal. Coils are about a foot wide, 1500 feet long, and about as thick as the final coin thickness. Each coil weighs close to 6,000 pounds.

How are blanks created?

A coil is hoisted onto a wheel that feeds into a blanking press. An operator cranks the wheel so the end of the metal sheet goes into the blanking press through a slot on the side. From the sheet, the blanking press punches out round, plain-surfaced disks called cut blanks.

After cutting a batch of blanks, the remaining metal (webbing), is chopped off and collected in a bin. By recycling the webbing to make new coinage strip, we ensure material is not wasted.

The blanks are now ready for the next steps: the creation of a planchet by softening, washing, and rimming the blanks' edges.

To soften the metal, blanks are placed in a furnace at temperatures over 700 degrees centigrade. Nickel blanks require the highest temperature. This process is called annealing during which, the molecules in the hard blanks are realigned to make the metal softer.

The high temperature of the annealing process creates a grayish discoloration on the surface of the metal. To make it bright and shiny, the metal needs to be cleaned.

17

From the furnace, the blanks drop into a quench tank to reduce the temperature. Next, the blanks travel through a huge cylindrical tube called the whirlaway.

Suspended high above the ground, these tubes tilt at a 45-degree angle toward the washing and drying station. As the blanks travel up the whirlaway toward the washer, excess liquid is drained.

After leaving the whirlaway, blanks are placed in a washing machine. Similar to the washing machine process you might have in your home, the blanks go through a series of cycles that soak and shake the blanks in various chemicals. This is to remove any oxides, tarnish, discoloration or contamination that remains after annealing.

Golden Dollars get a different treatment—they are burnished by steel shot resembling BBs.

The blanks are dried inside a tube and then poured out for the next treatment. In one hour, two tons of blanks can be annealed, washed, and dried.

In addition, the raised rim helps protect the coin's design. The highest point of any coin design is always lower than the coin's rim. Raising the rim hardens the edge and helps keep the coin from eroding. This also helps the coins to stack

If a reeded[15] edge is required, it is applied to the planchet during coining by a collar inside the coining press. Reeded edges help to identify coin's denomination.

The next stage of production is coining. This is the process of adding the design to the planchet.

Planchets travel to the stamping press through a press feed system. Most presses are fed planchets transported directly from upsetting machines running the same denomination. Each row of stamping presses runs the same coin denomination (for example, nickels) with the press force adjusted to the strength of the metal. Sensors are able to screen and detect flawed planchets.

To strike the metal, one die (known as the anvil) is held motionless and the other die (known as the hammer) strikes the planchet's surface. The anvil is usually a reverse (or tails) die and the hammer is the obverse (or heads).

The planchet's size, hardness, design intricacy, and relief determine the force needed to strike. Golden Dollar coins

---

[15] Reeded edge – A coin that contains a series of impressions on the edge of the coin.

18

require the greatest force, and pennies require the least force.

Fast-paced presses churn out 750 new coins every minute. The coins fill a collection box called a trap. An inspector checks the coins to see if they meet United States Mint quality standards.

Coins are compared to both visual and fill standards. Next, critical Statistical Process Control (SPC) and capability quality data are entered into the United States Mint's data collection system to track key processes.

If the coins pass inspection, the operator pulls the trap's lever. This discharges the coins onto a conveyor belt that transports them to the counting and bagging area.

An automatic counting machine, fitted with a sensor that detects correct products, counts the coins and drops them into large bags. "

True double die coins such as the 1955 Lincoln cent can command a significant value. True double die coins are rare. The 1955 double die Lincoln cent is the most pronounced error in the series to date.

The last two true double die Lincoln cent with date doubling was the 1969-S double die date valued in the tens of thousands and the 1972 valued in the hundreds.

Mint Striking Errors

Collectors and organizations dedicated to collecting coins regard mint striking errors as those created by the mint stamping process. Most of these coins command no significant value, especially those that have no date.

It is easy to get confused with an authentic double die and a mint striking error. Many coins in circulation appear doubled but the appearance of doubling is machine doubling and not actual die errors. Many of these coins appear on eBay as double dies and they are not.

Striking a coin with debris causing an indentation on the coin or actual debris stamped into the coin is a mint striking error. Although these coins are not very valuable, the mint makes every effort to catch and destroy these coins before they make it to circulation.

Coins can become broad struck when the collar that is holding the coin in place in the stamping process is missing. A broad struck coin is larger in diameter than the intended result.

Above is a broad struck dime.

Mint striking errors also include the misaligned coins minted and escape detection. There are thousands of coins that have been collected for their off center mintage. An off-center coin is the result of the holder of the planchet becoming loose and then the stamping is off center. Below is a 1997 off center Lincoln cent.

The most valuable of these coins are those that have a full date. A Lincoln cent that is even dramatically off center is valued around $2 without a date.

There are also coins that contain multiple portraits stamped on a coin that has been stamped outside of the collar and somehow finds its way back into the stamping process to be stamped a second time.

Found in coin guides specializing in mint striking errors are other classifications for mint striking errors

Variations

Variations are not mint errors in the technical sense. Coins minted by creating hubs and dies that are not exactly the same result in dates that can be compared as large to small, wide to thin etc.

Die variations have resulted in the 1960 large and small dated Lincoln cent production, and the 1982 large and small dated series both in copper and copper-zinc cents minted. All of these coins are intentional coin variations by the mint and they are not coin errors.

Some die variations are very valuable and others command no value difference between the coin variations of the same date and mintmark. Coins minted with die variations increase in value by the rarity of the number of coins minted.

Early dated coins have the most variety. Dies produced coins until they were unusable. In the same year, the mint could have produced coins with several features that are on some of the coins minted that are not on others. The value is based on the number of coins minted (or thought to be minted) with the lesser or greater number of a particular feature.

Coin Grading

Coin grading is subjective especially with mint state coins. Photographic coin guides that provide grading by denomination are helpful in determining the classification of a coin. We have added photographic grading to our coin guide of values.

Carbon spotting does detract from a coins value and the extent of the spotting many cause the coin classified as "corroded."

PCGS defines carbon spotting: *carbon spot*

A spot seen mainly on copper and gold coins, though also occasionally found on U.S. nickel coins (which are 75 percent copper) and silver coins (which are 10 percent copper). Carbon spots are brown to black spots of oxidation that range from minor to severe – some so large and far advanced that the coin is not graded because of environmental damage[16]

---

[16] PCGS carbon spot – from the PCGS web site

The coin above has severe carbon spotting reducing the value as an uncirculated sample.

Brilliant Uncirculated

PCGS defines BU: A generic term applied to any coin that has not been in circulation. Sometimes applied to Lincoln cent coins with little "brilliance" left, coins not brilliant are simply Uncirculated. [17]

Many sellers are reserved with the use of "uncirculated" and use "brilliant uncirculated" as a reference for brown Lincoln cents. The proper identification is "uncirculated or MS__.

The major encapsulation services list coins as Red/Brown, Brown, or Red for Lincoln cents.

Silver coins suffer carbon spotting and loss of luster and these coins are brilliant or circulated.

Choice Uncirculated

An Uncirculated coin grading MS-63 or MS-64. [18]

---

[17] PCS definition
[18] PCS definition

Chapter 2 – Large Cent Errors

Classifying coins of this era as an error coin or a variety coin is somewhat challenging since many of the "errors" may have been the conscientious decisions resulting in the using older dies to produce newer dated coins. For example, using a 1798 large cent die and modifying it to read 1799 is not honestly an error but the decision to change the die by the mint. These coins referred to as over-dates, or over mint mark (OMM) by collectors and some of them are extremely valuable.

Dr. William Shelton[19] spent a life- time cataloging all of the large cent variances resulting in the "S" (Shelton) denotations for large cent variations. Many coin auctions list large cents as the date followed by an "S" classification number representing the variation of the coin. Another well-known collector Walter Breen[20] joined with William Shelton to develop the "R" scale[21] used to reveal the number of large cents for any particular date. In high- end auctions the Shelton-Breen scale[22] classifies large cents along with any encapsulation grading. In some books, there is no "R" scale reference to the low-7 and high-7 designation leaving R-7 to mean 4-12 coins and the R-8 interpreted as 1-3 coins. There are nine levels on the Sheldon-Breen rarity scale:

R-8: only one coin known to exist

R-7 High: A coin excessively rare; 2 to 3 exist

R-7 Low: An extremely rare coin with 4 to 12 known

R-6: A very rare coin with 13 to 30 known

R-5: 31 to 75 coins exist, classifying it as rare

R-4: A very scarce coin with 76 to 200 coins

R-3: With 201 to 500 estimated coins

R-2: A coin that is not common, with 501 to 1250 coins in existence

R-1: With at least 1251 coins remaining, this is a common coin.

Dr Shelton was the pioneer in developing the foundation for the present day coin grading system. It was Dr Shelton the designated coin grades by using a numbering system from 1

---

[19] William Shelton was one of the pioneers in developing coin-grading systems.

[20] Walter Breen- renowned collector and coin expert.

[21] R Scale – the number of coins minted.

[22] Shelton-Breen scale developed to classify the large cent rarities.

23

through 70 that has been converted to present day fair, about good, good, very good, fine, very fine, extra fine, about uncirculated, and Mint State (MS) grading systems of MS60 through MS70. It is impossible for the novice collector to grade any coin with an MS designation because there are no books available that can exactly describe the grading technique in recording the numbers of nicks, scratches, and surface blemishes that place an uncirculated coin in a specific MS grade. Sometimes the grading panel members at the encapsulation services cannot agree on a particular MS grade and the coin usually obtains the lower grade. There are numerous examples of small and large date varieties, however, these are most likely the result of the die makers and perhaps should not be called errors but instead variations. It is obvious that back in the 1880's many dies produced subsequent years of coins by modifying the date. So many variations of large cents by date exist that it would take the dedication of someone to author a book to reveal all of them. There were tall dates, short dates, wide letters, slanted dates, use of obverses and reverses of different dates, and variations in the design that require careful cataloging.

Realized at auction is the true value of error large cent coins and the demand for them.

Pictured above is an 1807 over 1806 large cent

24

Use great care in determining a genuine large cent error. When considering bidding at auction or on the internet take care to avoid purchasing a fake or a coin that is not truly an error.

Some of the large cent error coins can command a remarkable amount of money at auction. An 1801 "three errors" coin (one stem, 1/1000, UNITED) sold on the internet for $275,000 in very good condition. The coin photographs presented well and the three errors clearly identified. A high-end collector desiring to put a collection of large cents together would most likely strive to obtain all of the variations and thus be willing to pay a lot of money to obtain one coin error of every type.

Any of the rarer large cent error coins in about uncirculated or better conditions are likely to produce coin values well over $100,000. Research into past and present auctions has revealed a true rarity with these coins in the highest grades. Below is a detailed listing of the large cent error coin sold at high- end auctions.

1797 reverse of 1797 stems (ANACS, G6, $184-345) (NGC F, $862) (PCGS AU58, $5,462) (PCGS MS64, $16,100)

1797 reverse of 1797 no stems (NGC, G, $322)

1797 reverse of 1795 (AG3, $488)

1798 second hairstyle (ANACS, G4, corroded, $56)

1799 over 1798 (PCGS Fair, $1,955) (PCGS G6, $12,650) (PCGS VG8, $8,050) (PCGS VG10, $10,925)

1799 over 1798 over date (PCGS VF35, $48,875)

1800 over 1798 over date (NGC G4, $207) (NGC VG10, $5,462) (NGC F15, $138-$875) (NGC VF25, $1,035-$1,995) (NCG AU58 cleaned, $4,025-$8,050)
 (ANACS MS65, $92,000)

1800 over 1799

1801 three errors (one stem, 1/1000, UNITED) (PCGS VG8, $529) (NGC VF30, $3,220-$3,737.50) (PCGS AU53, $14,950) (NGC AU58, $5,175) (NGC MS63, $138,000)

1801 1/100 over 1/1000 (PCGS VG10, $432) (NGC VF35, 1,380) (PCGS EF40, $2,530) (PCGS AU50, $3,594)

1803 Small Date Small Fraction (PCGS VF35 $547) (PCGS CAC EF45, $1,610)

1803 Small Date Large Fraction (PCGS VG8, $173) (PCGS VF35 $633) (NGC AU50, $1,495) (NGC MS64, $16,100)

1804 broken dies re-strike (NGC MS64, $1,380) (PCGS MS66, $1,840)

1807 large 7 over 6 (NGC VG8, $2,990) (NGC VF30, $460-$1,495) (PCGS MS65, $86,250)
1807 small 7 over 6 (NGC VF25, $11,500- $27,500) (PCGS AU55, $161,000)
1807 small 7 over 6 blunt 1 (raw VF30, $3,960)
1811 over 1810 (ANACS AG3, $60-$66) (NGC G6, $250-$374) (ANACS F12, $286-$488) (PCGS VF35, $3,450) (PCGS EF 45, $3,222) (PCGS AU50, $6,600-$11,500)
1819 over 1818 (NGC EF45, $345) (ANACS AU50, $400-$546) (NGC MS64, $1,725)
1820 over 1819 (ANACS G6, $35) (ANACS VG8, $37) (NGC VF25, $149.50) (NGC AU55, $833.75)
1823 over 1822 none located
1839 over 1836 none located
1844 over 1881 (PCGS VG10, $125.50) (ANACS F12, $95) (ANACS VF20, $109.25-$161) (NGC EF45, $345) (PCGS AU55, $1,495) (PCGS MS64, $29,000)
1851 over 1881 (PCGS VF30, $126.50) (NGC EF45, $207-$373.75) (NGC AU58, $410.50) (PCGS MS65, $1,725-$4,312.50) (NGC MS66, $3,220-$5.750)
1855 slanted 5's (PR65, $715)
1856 slanted 5 (PCGS AU50, $126.50)
1857 small date (PCGS PR65, $8,050)

Chapter 3 – Small Cents
Flying Eagle 1856-1858
There are a few flying-eagle cent errors listed below.
Because of the short mintage of the flying eagle cent, errors
are limited to three years of mintage.

Pictured above is an 1856 flying eagle cent obverse and reverse
Below is a listing of Flying Eagle coins that discovered
through researching auction sites.
1857 struck on thin planchet (PCGS MS63, $3800) 2016
1857 Double die obverse (PCGS MS65, $1100)
1858 small date (NGC EF40, $84, $127.50) (PCGS MS64,
$1495)
1858 large date (NGC EF40, $138) (PCGS MS64, $1092.50)
1858/7 (NGC VF30, $345) (ANACS EF40, $299) (PCGS
AU50, $850-$1,100) (NGC AU58, $3,500) (NGC MS64,
$10,350-$20,700) (NGC MS65, $27,600)
Ever wonder where all of the 1856 flying eagle cents went?
Walter Breen, noted collector and well-respected coin expert
published the following distribution of 1856 Flying Eagle
Cents:
264 (or more) to Congressmen
200 to Representative S.D. Campbell
102 to Secretary of the Treasury James Guthrie
62 to Senators
4 to President Franklin Pierce
2 to the Mint Cabinet
Additional pieces were given to dignitaries and others"

Indian Cents 1859-1909

In 1864, the mint issued two varieties, coins without an "L" on the ribbon and coins dated 1864 with an "L" on the ribbon. The 1864 with the L on the ribbon is the more valuable of the two coins in part because in the lowest grades the L disappears.

The 1867 Indian cent mintage included coins discovered with the 67 over 67. This error is valued over $20,000 in mint state conditions.

In 1873, there were two types of Indian cents minted. One 1873 version has a closed three and the other an open three. There is a distinct difference between the open and closed three so that it appears clearly without a magnifying glass. There are examples of 1873 Indian cents with doubled "LIBERTY". The double liberty Indian cent of 1873 commanded the highest selling price of any error coin in this series that was located. The double liberty coin sold for $69,000 in MS65 condition.

The 1888 Indian cent production from using a die from 1887 modified for 1888 mintage resulted in the eight punched in the die over the seven. These coins can obtain a value between $400 in good and $8,000 in proof condition. Anyone believing that they have an 1888 over seven should send the coin to PCGS, ANACS, or NCG for verification.

There are many types of errors for Indian cents encapsulated and sold at high-end auctions. It is nearly impossible to list and catalog all the errors that have resulted in missed-aligned dies, loose collars, and incorrect planchets.

A 1905 Indian cent struck on a quarter-eagle planchet sold at a Heritage Auction[23] for $253,000.

An 1863 Indian cent encapsulated by PCGS that was broad struck[24] listed on eBay at a starting price of $400 but it did not sell.

Below is a listing of Indian Cent error coins that have been located from various auctions.

1858 small letters DDR 3 (PCGS MS64, $1380)
1860 pointed bust (PCGS MS66, $12,650-$15,525)

---

[23] Heritage Auctions – A well -known and major live and internet auction house.
[24] Broad struck – A coin struck with out the collar that holds the coin in place. The coin impression minted in the center of the coin with material spreading around the coin giving a framed look.

1864 L on the ribbon (PCGS EF45, $230-$276)
1864 without the L (NCG MS65, $299- $1,265 Red)
1864/64 (NGC G4, $35) 2015
1864/64 "L" on ribbon (NCG VG8, $94)
1865 fancy 5 (PCGS MS66, $12,650- $28,750)
1866 6 over 6 (ANACS G4, $32) 2015
1867/67 (IGC G6, $42) (PCGS F12, $253) (ANACS VG10,
$144) (PCGS AU55, $700) (NGC MS65, $23,000-$24,380)
1868 DDO (NGC MS65 red, $920)
1869/69 repunched date (ANACS G4, $85) 2015
1870 DDO (NGC G4, $51.75) (ANACS VG8, $90) 2015
1870 DDO and DDR (ANACS MS60, $431.25)
1870 DDR (ANACS VG8 $89) 2015
1872 DDO (NGC MS65, $56) 2014
1873 closed 3 (ANACS G4, $105) (NGC EF45, $172.50)
(PCGS MS66, $16,675)
1873 closed 3 DDO (ANACS VG8, $230) (ANACS VF35,
$184) (NGC MS63, $1,035)
1873 open 3 (H, NGC EF45, $138)
1873 double "LIBERTY" (NGC G4, $240) (PCGS VG10,
$632) (PCGS VF20, $833.75) (PCGS AU55, $3,565) (PCGS
MS65, $23,000-$69,000) (PCGS MS64, $32,200) 2015
1877 stuck on a Venezuela one-centavo planchet (H, NGC
MS61, $21,850)
1887 DDO (PCGS AU53, $370) 2014
1888 8 over 7 (PCGS G4, $126.50) (PCGS VG30, $1800)
(PCGS VF30, $6,325) (PCGS EF45, $12,075-$12,600)
1894 double date (NGC VG10, $72) (PCGS MS65, $10,500-
$12,650)
1897 over 1889 none located
1891 DDR – 001 (ANACS MS63, $184)
1905 Indian cent struck on a quarter-eagle planchet –
Heritage auctions $253,000

Lincoln Cents 1909-date

Some mint errors are well known and others are documented but not as popular. Lincoln cent error coins have the highest number of encapsulation than any other coin series to date. The prices realized for Lincoln error coins are the highest among any other denomination, especially in grades of mint state.

The first year of mintage provided a variation in with the San Francisco mintage yielding an S over S mintage. The S over S mintage is not rare to the date itself since this coin sells for the same price as the 1909-S with no doubling. There are some examples of 1909 VDB coins with doubling on the obverse that have been discovered and encapsulated and they can sell from several hundred dollars to several thousand dollars depending upon the grade.

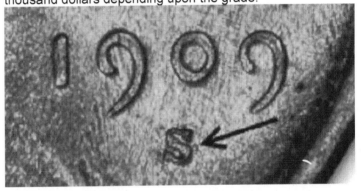

Pictured is a 1909-S/S coin

In 1922, the Denver mint used the dies on the obverse until the D no longer pressed into the coin resulting in a 1922 coins without the D. If there had been minting of the 1922 coin at the Philadelphia mint that year, it would have been a challenge to distinguish where the coins originated.

Pictured above is a 1922 error cent

In 1922, four dies produced error coins for the 1922. The 1922-D full mint- mark, the 1922-D weak D die set, the no D strong reverse, and the no D weak reverse. The 1922 no D coin is valued in a range of $300 in the lowest grade to over $5,000 in MS60 conditions. Some of these coins in MS64 and MS65 have sold between $40,000 and $50,000 at auction.

Pictured above a 1943 Lincoln cent struck on a bronze planchet.

There are some examples of 1943 and 1943-S minted Lincoln cents struck on bronze planchets out in the collecting world. Bronze 1943 samples sell in excess of $200,000.

1944-S Zinc cent

The Lincoln cent above is a 1944-S error coin minted on a zinc planchet. This coin sold for $373,750 on the Heritage auction site July 31, 2008. There are examples of a 1944-D bronze Lincoln cent with the D over S minted errors.

The most sought after Lincoln cent error coin has always been the 1955 double die. This is a true mint error coin with a very clear doubling of the date. At auction, a 1955 double die NGC MS-66 Red sold at Bowers & Merena Galleries "The Rarities Sale", July 31, 2002, Lot 63, illustrated, for $46,000[25]. There are thousands of 1955 double die cents sold at auction every day for collectors to obtain and enjoy and most at reasonable prices for the rarity of the coin.

---

[25] Data from coin facts

Pictured above is the 1955 double die cent

Only two known examples of the 1958 double-die cent exist and both of them are PCGS MS65 specimens valued over $140,000. The doubling on the obverse of the 1958 DDO cent is on the motto "IN GOD WE TRUST" and the word "LIBERTY".

Not mint errors, but die varieties, the 1960 Lincoln cent series contains small dates and large dates. The small dated 1960 coins are generally valued at $6 for the 1960 small date in MS65 and $4 for the 1960-D small date in MS65 condition.

One of the most valuable more recent Lincoln cent double-die is the 1969-S. This coin can sell in excess of $50,000 in MS conditions since the number of these coins discovered has been extremely limited. The doubling in this coin is clear in LIBERTY, IN GOD WE TRUST, and the 1969-S date. Collectors need to be careful not to confuse machine doubling with the actual hub error minted coins. Machine doubling will show some letters and numbers to contain some flashing contributed from the pressing of the coin in the dies.

Pictured above is a 1969-S Lincoln cent double die. Note the extreme doubling of the word "LIBERTY."

The mint produced variations of the 1970-S Lincoln cent with a small date and a large dated version. The small dated version is valued between $50 and $100 depending upon the MS grade. The large date 1970-S coin is the standard issued coin, and it commands no extra value in circulated condition. The seven in the coin that serves as a reference point for differentiating the large version to the small version date. Drawing a line along the top of the date the seven, the small dated seven will be slightly below the rest of the date. It may be possible to locate the 1970-S low 7 cent in circulation since the two versions are difficult to distinguish at a glance.

Above is a photograph of a 1970-S small date 7. The 7 is just below the line of where the 9 and the 0 is touching.

Some proof variations occurred in 1979 were the filled S in some sets. These variations do not command any significant value and are common in proof sets.

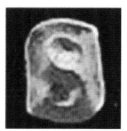

In 1981, the mint produced a filled type S in proof sets shown above as well as a normal S mint. The non- filled S minted coin is valued at $45 while the filled S mint is the norm.

Contrary to any belief, the 95% copper Lincoln cents did not end in 1964, it ended in 1982. The 1982 mintage is a mix of copper and copper clad coinage.

In 1982, the mint produced seven different Lincoln cents. With 95% copper content, the mint produced a 1982 small date, a 1982 large date, and a 1982-D large date. The composition of the Lincoln cent changed to 97% zinc and 3% copper with the minting of a 1982 large date, a 1982 small date, a 1982-D large date and a 1982-D small date. A collector aspiring to collect these variations can purchase the whole set for under $10 in uncirculated condition. The zinc in the coin shows by cutting a cent in half or removing the copper top layer of the cent.

In 1983, the mint released a percentage of coins with a doubling of the reverse. The doubling is the strongest in the word "ONE" but most of the double lettering on the reverse is legible by eyesight. These coins will yield between $400 and $750 in various MS grades.

A recent double die cent is the 1995. The doubling on these coins is not as apparent as other double die Lincoln cent coins. The doubling occurs in "LIBERTY" and "In GOD" with the doubling of liberty more pronounced. This coin sells for under $100 in mint state condition.

In 1997, some Lincoln cents appeared to have a double ear. The doubling occurs above the ear with hair doubled and with ear lobe. Some collectors dispute this coin as a double die cent and not noted in some coin guides. There is an example of a PCGS MS65 double ear coin that sold at auction for over $195.

Becoming an expect DDO and DDR numismatist has its rewards since there are collectors that are willing to pay

$100 of more for these coins in encapsulation. Thousands of brilliant uncirculated rolls of Lincoln cents in the market maybe searched for some of these DDO and DDR finds. Before sending any DDO or DDR coin to an encapsulation service, the collector should be sure the grade and the cost of encapsulation will yield a benefit.

A Lincoln cent obverse minted with the reverse of a dime sold auction for $138,000. Pictured below:

Collectors refer to this type of error as a mule.

No other coin series has as many error coins as the Lincoln cent series. The vast number of one-cent coins minted and the refurbishing of the dies have created thousands of RPM's. The number of errors and variations are numerous and new discoveries will continue as collectors search through their coins.

Lincoln errors include a vast number of samples minted on dime planchets. Below is a long list of error coins with the encapsulated grades and price ranges from completed auctions.

1909 VDB DDO (PCGS MS64, $230-$1,438) (PCGS MS65, $489-$4,888) (PCGS MS66, $747-$12075)

1909-S over S Horizontal S (ANACS VG10, $89) (NGC MS63, $299-$345) (NGC MS64, $518) (PCGS MS65, $1006) (PCGS MS66, $2,070)

1911 D over D (PCGS VF, no bids)

1917 DDO (PCGS G04 $69) (PCGS F12 $144) (raw EF40, $978) (PCGS MS66, $25,300-$28,750)

1920 struck on an Argentina 10 cent (NGC AU55, $500) 2015

1922 no D or partial D (PCGS G6, $250) (ANACS VG8, $800) (PCGS AU55, $4113) (PCGS MS63, $2500-$14,000)

1925-S over S (PCGS F15, $50) 2016

1927 D over D (PCGS MS64, $660) 2014

1930-S over S (PCGS MS64, $86) (NGC MS66, $225) 2016

1934-D over D (PCGS F12, $55) 2016

1935 DDO (PCGS MS63, $248)
1936 DDO proof type I
1936 proof type II DDO (PCGS MS66, $5,400-$5,750)
1936 DDO 2 (PCGS MS65, $3500) (PCGS MS66, $11,500-$21,850) note* there are a few degrees of doubling for this year.
1936 DDO die 3 (PCGS MS65, $1700)
1938 D over D (NGC MS65, $40) (ANACS MS65, $21) 2014
1938-S triple S (ANACS MS65, $26-$65) (NGC MS65, $72-$129) (NGC MS66, $39-$100) (NGC MS67, $100-$135) 2016
1938-S over S (NGC VF25, $112) (ANACS MS65, $29-$300) (NGC MS66, $42-$225) (NGC MS67, $160-$230) 2016
1939-S over S (MS65, $30) 2016
1939 DDO (PCGS MS66, $575-$960)
1940-D over D (ANACS MS64, $23) 2014
1940-S S over S (ANACS MS64, $74) (ANACS MS66, $132.25)
1940-S triple S (ANACS MS64, $26-$79) (ANACS MS66, $58)
1941 struck on a Panama cent (PCGS MS65, $4995) 2015
1941 DDO (PCGS VF20, $65) (PCGS MS65, $719-$6,325) (PCGS-NGC MS66, $5,175-$5,750)
1942 struck on a think brass planchet (ANACS VF30, $130) 2015
1942 struck on an Ecuador 10 centavos (NGC VF35, $1880) 2015
1942 struck on a dime planchet (PCGS MS63, $6200) (ANACS AU58, $11750) 2015
1942 DDO (ANACS EF45, $38) (ANACS AU50, $19)
1942-D D over D (PCGS MS65, $300) 2015
1942-S DDO (PCGS MS64, $172.50) (PCGS MS65, $184)
1942-S S over S (ANACS EF45, $77) (ANACS MS65, $31) (NGC MS66, $287.50) (ANACS MS66, $38-$42) (ANACS MS67, $86-$225) 2016
1942-S DDR (ANACS MS63, $146)
1942-S triple S (NGC MS65, $345) (PCGS CAC MS66, $546) (NGC MS66, $288-$299) (NGC MS67, $432) 2016
1943 struck on a dime planchet – (PCGS VF25, $1750) (NGC AU50, $15275) 2015
1943 overstruck on a Cuba 1 centavo (PCGS MS62, $38,200) 2015
1943 struck on bronze planchent (PCGS AU58, $218,500)
1943 struck on Curacao 25 cent planchet (NGC EF40, $14,950) (NGC AU58, $11,500)

1943 D over D (PCGS MS65, $805- $2,530) (PCGS MS67, $4,500-$21,275)
1943-S DDO (PCGS MS67, 2325) 2015
1943-S struck on a bronze planchet (PCGS VF35, $207,000)
1943-S struck on a dime planceht (PCGS AU50, $3525) (PCGS AU55, $8825-14100) (PCGS AU58, $4250) 2016
1944 struck on a brass planchet (NGC MS63, $425) 2015
1944 struck on a dime planchet (PCGS XF40, $3050) 2015
1944 struck on a Netherlands 25 cent (PCGS MS63, $5200-7635) 2014
1944 struck on a Philippines 5 centavos (PCGS MS62, $6463) 2015
1944-D struck on a dime planchet (PCGS MS65, $4400) 2015
1944-D over D (ANACS MS60, $11) (PCGS MS67, $2200) 2016
1944 D with S located below the D (PCGS $29)
1944 D over S (PCGS MS66, $2,200- $16,100) (PCGS MS65, $5,100-$5,462.50)
1944-D struck on zinc coated 1943 cent (ANACS AU50, $34,500)
1944-D on zinc planchet (NGC MS63, $115,000)
1944-S on zinc planchet (NGC MS66, $373,750)
1945 struck on a Netherlands East Indies (NGC MS64, $765) 2015
1945 struck on an Ethiopia centavo (NGC MS62, $1645) 2015
1945 D over D (ANACS MS60, $25) 2014
1945-S struck on a dime planchet (NGC XF40, $560) 2015
1945-S struck over Netherlands East Indies (NGC AU58, $7050) 2015
1945-S DDO (ANACS MS67, $167)
1945-S over S (ANACS, $150) 2016
1946 D over D (ANACS MS64, $65) (NGC MS67, $75) 2016
1946-D struck on a dime planchet (ANACS AU50, $300) 2015
1946-S over S (ANACS MS63, $40) (ANACS MS64, $37) (ANACS MS66, $29) 2016
1947 DDO (PCGS MS64, $250) 2014
1947-S over S (ANACS MS66, $28) 2016
1948-S over S DDO (ANACS MS65, $173)
1948-S over S (ANACS MS66, $69) (ANACS MS66, $69) 2016
1949-D over D (PCGS MS64, $75) (PCGS MS64, $440) 2016
1949-S DDO (NGC MS65, $20) 2016

1949-S over S (ANACS MS65, $36-$75) 2016
1950-S over S (PCGS MS65, $35-$41) (ANACS MS66, $21-$78) 2016
1951 DDO (PCGS PR64, $54-$79)
1951-D DDO (PCGS MS63, $45) 2014
1951-D over D (ANACS AU58, $12) (ANACS MS65, $69) 2016
1951-D triple D (ANACS MS64, $75)
1952-D over D (SEGS, MS65, $15) 2016
1951-D over S (PCGS, MS66, $230-$300), NGC MS67, $2350) 2014
1952-S struck on a dime planchet (NGC XF45, $1725) 2015
1952-S over S (PCGS MS67, $117) 2016
1953 DDO (PCGS PR66, $161-$267) (PCGS PR67, $230)
1953-D struck on a dime planchet (PCGS AU53, $920) 2015
1953 D over D (PCGS MS65, $79-$85) (NGC MS65, $23) 2016
1953-S over S (ANACS MS65, $28) 2016
1954-D DDO (ANACS MS65, $55) 2016
1954 D over D (ANACS MS65, $69) 2016
1954 D/D/D (ANACS MS65, $130-$350) 2016
1954 D/D/D (PCGS MS64, $50-$65) (ANACS MS65, $52-$350) 2016
1954-S over S (ANACS MS64, $14) (ANACS MS65, $28-$69) (ANACS MS66, $16-$22) 2016
1955 struck on Venezuela 25 cent (ANACS MS60, $1610) 2015
1955 DDO (PCGS AU55, $1800) not double date 2015
1955 DDR and DDO (ANACS PR65, $25)
1955 Double die date sold at Bowers and Merena Galleries graded PCGS MS66 $46,000
1955-D over D (ANACS MS 65, $22) (ANACS MS66, $23-$69) 2016
1955-D DDO (ANACS MS64, $42)
1955-S S over S (ANACS MS63, $48) (ANACS MS64, $48-$92) (ANACS MS65, $42-$127) (NGC MS66, $60) (ANACS MS66, $25) 2016
1955-S triple S (PCGS MS64, $32-$92) (ANACS MS65, $127) (NGC MS66, $54-$79) (ANACS MS67, $79) 2016
1956-D struck on Roosevelt dime (PCGS AU58, $2590) 2015
1956-D over S (NCG, MS66, $55) 2016
1956 D/D/S (ANACS MS64, $40) 2014
1956-D over D (ANACS MS65, $35-$56) (PCGS MS67, $1293) 2016

1956-D triple D (ANACS MS65, $59-$184)
1957 struck on a 1957 dime (PCGS AU58, $3450) 2015
1957 struck on a dime planchet (PCGS MS63, $825) 2015
1957-D struck on a dime planchet (NGC XF40, $345) 2015
1957 D over D (ANACS MS65, $29-$100) 2014
1957-D triple D (ANACS MS65, $80)
1958 struck on a dime blank (NGC MS63, $940) 2015
1958 struck on a Cuba centavo (NGC AU58, $1575) 2015
1958-D over D (ANACS MS64, $11) 2014
1958-D Triple D (ANACS MS66, $32) 2016
1959 DDO (ANACS MS62, $14)
1959-D triple D (ANACS MS63, $154) (PCGS MS65, $26-$184) (PCGS MS66, $30-$116)
1960 struck on a dime planchet (NGC MS60, $374) 2015
1960 Triple DDO (NGC PR65, $80)
1960 DDO Small over Large date (PCGS PR65, $299) (PCGS PR66, $276) (NGC PR67, $385), (PCGS PR68, $4600)
1960 DDO Large over Small Date (PCGS PR67, $300-$400), (PCGS PR68, $603-$1,006), (PCGS PR69, $7475)
1960-D DDO Small over Large Date (PCGS PR66, $276) 2014
1960-D DDO Large over Small Date (NGC PR64, $109) (NGC PR65, $138-$219) (NGC PR66, $161-253) (NGC PR67, $253-483)
1960-D D over D Small over Large Date (PCGS MS64, $155) (PCGS MS65, $130-$376) 2016
1960-D D over D Large over Small Date (PCGS MS66, $676) 2016
1961 struck on a dime planchet (NGC MS63, $1700) 2015
1961-D struck on a 1960-D small date (PCGS AU58, $4600) 2016
1961-D over D (ANACS MS65, $105) 2014
1961-D over Horizontal D (PCGS MS64, $25-$50) 2016
1962 struck on a Philippine 10 centavo (NGC MS65, $575) 2015
1962 struck on a dime planchet (NGC MS65, $3825) 2015
1962 ANACS Proof DDO
1963-D DDO (PCGS MS64, $38) 2011
1964 struck on a dime planchet (ANACS MS64, $5750) 2015
1964 SMS (PCGS MS67, $11,500)
1964 DDO (ANACS MS65, $115) 2014
1964 DDR (NGC MS62, $34)
1964-D struck on a dime planchet (NGC MS64, $597) 2015

1965 struck on a clad dime planchet (PCGS MS64, $550) 2015
1965 struck on a 1965 dime (NGC MS65, $1765) 2015
1966 DDO (PCGS AU58, $25)
1966 staple embedded (NGC MS62, $1150) 2015
1966 struck on a dime planchet (PCGS MS65, $382) 2015
1967 DDO (NGC MS60, $47) 2015
1967 struck on a dime planchet (PCGS AU58, $520) 2015
1968 Struck on a Canadian dime planchet (ANACS MS62, $400) 2015
1968-D over D (NGC MS65, $38) (PCGS MS65, $165) 2016
1968-S struck on a dime planchet (PCGS MS64, $299) 2015
1969 struck on a Canadian dime planchet (NGC MS62, $3820) 2015
1969 double struck on a dime (NGC MS62, $3820) 2015
1969-D struck on a dime planchet (NGC MS60, $275) 2015
1969-S double die obverse (PCGS MS63, $57,500-$86,250)
1970 struck on a dime planchet (ANACS MS64, $368) 2015
1970-S large date struck on dime planchet (PCGS PR64, $2990) 2015
1970-S large date DDO (PCGS PR63, $28) light version
1970-S DDO small date
1970-S DDO large date (PCGS MS63, $5,750) (PCGS MS64, $10,500) (PCGS MS65, $5,462)
1970-S over S (ANACS MS63, $74) (ANACS MS64, $26-$38) 2016
1971 DDO (PCGS MS64, $488-$634) (PCGS MS66, $10,500)
1971-D struck on a dime planchet (PCGS MS62, $860) 2015
1971-S DDO (NGC PR65, $150) (NGC PR67, $603-$805)
1972 DDO (PCGS MS64, $42-$427) (PCGS MS65, $26-$431) (PCGS MS67 red, $5,400-$5,750)
1972 72 over72 (ANACS MS64, $59-$460) (ANACS MS65, $460-$662) (PCGS MS66, $718-$1,122) (NGC MS67, $2,245)
1972-D over D (ANACS MS66, $27) 2016
1974 struck on a dime planchet (NGC MS66, $382) 2015
1975 struck on a dime planchet (NGC MS61, $305) 2015
1977 struck on a 1977 dime (NGC MS67, $2100) 2015
1977 struck on a dime planchet (ANACS MS64, $415) 2015
1978 struck on a dime planchet (ANACS MS62, $665) 2015
1979-D Lincoln cent struck on a dime planchet (ANACS MS65, $575) 2015
1980 struck on a dime planchet (PCGS MS64, $765) 2015

1980-D struck on a dime planchet (NGC MS63, $260) 2015
1980 DDO (PCGS MS65, $1500) 2016
1981 struck on a 198x dime (PCGS MS66, $1050) 2015
1981-D struck on a dime planchet (NGC MS64, $300) 2015
1982 large date stuck in dime planchet (NGC MS65, $575) 2015
1982 small date stuck in dime planchet (PCGS MS64, $431) 2015
1982 DDO large date die 2 (ANACS MS65, $21)
1982 DDO small date copper
1982 DDO large date copper
1982-D DDO larger date copper
1982 DDO small date zinc/copper plated
1982-D DDO small date zinc/copper plated
1982 DDO large date zinc/copper plated
1982-D DDO larger date zinc/copper plated
1983 struck on an unplated planchet (NGC MS66, $282) 2015
1983 struck on a copper planchet (PCGS AU55, $16,500) 2014
1983 DDO (NGC MS64, $42-$70)
1983 DDR (PCGS MS64, $213) (NGC MS68, $3,220)
1984 stuck on a dime planchet (PCGS MS62, $600) 2015
1984 DDO (ANACS MS62, $51) (PCGS MS65, $219) (PCGS MS66, $495) (PCGS MS67, $630-$805)
1985 struck on a dime planchet (PCGS MS65, $765) 2015
1986 struck on a dime planchet (ANACS MS61, $225) 2015
1987 struck on a dime planchet (PCGS MS65, $940) 2015
1988 struck on a dime planchet (NGC MS64, $390) 2015
1989 struck on a dime planchet (PCGS MS66, $450) 2015
1989 struck on a 1988 dime (NGC MS65, $2115) 2015
1990 struck on a dime planchet (NGC MS64, $650) 2015
1990 no S proof (PCGS PR66, $5,400-$5,750)
1991 struck on a dime planchet (ANACS MS65, $881) 2015
1992 struck on a 1992 dime planchet (ANACS MS63, $1438) 2015
1993 struck on a dime planchet (NGC MS66, $460) 2015
1994 struck on a dime planchet (PCGS MS66, $700) 2015
1994 DDR (NGC MS64, $79)
1995 struck on a dime planchet (PCGS MS64, $882) 2015
1995 DDO (PCGS MS67, $69-$74) (PCGS MS68, $79)
1996 DDO (NGC MS61, $89) 2015
1996-D struck on a zinc planchet (PCGS MS64, $130) 2015
1997 struck on a dime planchet (PCGS MS63, $650) 2015

1997 double ear (PCGS MS65, $195.50)
1998 struck on dime planchet (PCGS MS67, $430) 2015
1998 struck on a 1998 dime (NGC MS65, $825) 2015
1999 stuck on a dime planchet (PCGS MS65, $680) 2015
1999 struck on a 1999 dime (NGC MS67, $950) 2015
2000 struck on 2000 dime planchet (NGC MS66, $805) 2015
2000 struck on a dime planchet (NGC MS67, $650) 2015
2001 struck on a Sacagawea dollar (PCGS MS66, $32,250) 2015
2001 struck on a dime planchet (PCGS MS64, $650) 2015
2001 struck on a 2000 dime (NGC MS63, $1645) 2015
2006 DDO (PCGS MS65, $50) 2016
2009 formative years – rail splitter with a 6th finger (ANACS MS66, $95)
2014 DDO (PCGS MS64, $150) 2016

Chapter 4– Two Cent 1864-1873

There are very few coin errors in the market place concerning two- cent pieces.

The 1864 mintage produced small motto and large motto coins. The small motto coins are the most valuable realizing $3,000 for an encapsulated coin in MS64 condition and as much as $32,000 for a coin graded by the top three grading companies in MS65 condition.

There is only one double die two-cent piece that has been widely recognized. The 1867 piece circulated with a doubling on the obverse and a collector that desires to obtain a low graded sample can purchase an encapsulated coin for under $100.

Pictured above is an 1864 two-cent piece

In 1873, the mint yielded coins with a closed three. These are rare and can bring upwards of $50,000 at auction in proof condition, which is the only production the mint released.

1864 large motto (NGC AU58, $977.50) (NGC MS65, $345-$1,624) (PCGS MS66, $3,047-$3,738)

1864 large motto rotated dies (NGC AU50, $99)

1864 small motto (PCGS MS64 $2,300-$3,000) (NGC MS65, $852-$21,850) (PCGS MS66, $32,200)

1867 DDO (ANACS VG10, $60) (ANACS VF30, $126.50) (NGC MS62, $2,530) (ANACS AU50, $632.50) (PCGS MS64, $6,175)

Chapter 5– Three Cent 1851-1873

The three- cent piece was another one of the US Mint's short- lived series.

The content of silver in these coins was 75% with 25% copper. Production of these coins reduced the shortage of coins created by the gold rush in California. The lack of popularity rendered the coin to discontinuation and replaced by the three-cent –nickel.

In 1863, coins resulted in using dies of the 1862 version causing the three striking over the two. This error date is restricted to the proof issues in 1863.

Any date in this series that is in MS65 condition or higher is likely to realize in excess of $10,000 regardless of containing an error or not.

Pictured above is an 1856 three cent silver

The difficulty with collecting this series would be to locate the dates from 1863 through 1873. In good condition, these coins will sell between $250 and $300.

Below is a couple of error coins located from a search of completed auctions.

1862 2 over 1 (PCGS MS64, $13,800) (PCGS MS66, $1,500-$4,448) (NGC MS67, $3,000-$3,450)

1883 3 over 2 (NGC PR66, $6,900- $8,944) (NGC PR67, $13,225)

Chapter 6 – Three-Cent Nickel 1865-1889

Series completion requires devoting time to look for the coins for a collection. A few dates would set a collector back some cash. The 1883, 1884, 1885, 1886, and 1887 dates are the rarest in the collection with coin values starting between $200 and $300 in good condition.

The only date that contains error coins is the 1873. The mint produced one version with a closed three and another with a normal open three.

Pictured above is an 1885 three-cent nickel

Although this coin appears to be silver, it is not. The composition of this coin is 75% copper and 25% nickel. The coins are nick named "three cent nickel" verses a three-cent piece. The mint produced two versions of the 1873 date with a closed and an open 3.

1873 open 3 (PCGS MS65, $3,750-$4,025)
1873 closed 3 (PCGS MS65, $2,700) (PCGS MS66, $2,700-$3,680) (NGC PR67, $3,300-$4,300)

Chapter 7 – Nickels 1866 to date

The first nickel minted in 1866 started the series and the nickel was on its way to become a yearly mint release to this day. The nickel permanently replaced the three-cent piece after 1889.

The Shield Nickel 1866-1883

Even though the US Mint was issuing three-cent pieces, it was not enough to satisfy the demand for coinage in circulation. The first nickel minted contained rays that circled the large five on the coin. In 1867, this version and a version of the nickel without the rays became part of the mintage. The version of the nickel with the rays ended after 1867. The 1867 version with the rays is more valuable than the version without the rays especially in grades of MS.

1868 DDR (NGC MS64, $547) 2015
1868 DDO (PCGS Genuine, $127) 2015
1870 DDR (PCGS XF45, $150) 2015
1870/70 DDO (NGC VF, $224) 2015
1872 DDO (ANACS PR62, $299) 2015
1872 CAMEO (PCGS PR66, $1265) 2015
1873 DDO (PCGS Genuine, $280) 2015
1873 DDO closed 3 (NGC MS62, $650) 2015
1874 DDO (NGC MS63, $355) 2015
1875 DDO (ANACS AU55, $140) 2015

In 1873, there were two mintages, one with an open 3 and one with a closed 3. Both 1873 types are valued about the same in all conditions.

The 1878 issue is in proof only and these coins are valued upwards of $2,500. In 1879, the mint issued some coins with the nine over eight. These are very scarce and can attain a value in the millions.

Shield nickels in the lowest conditions are affordable with prices between $15 and $50 each with a few exceptions. The keys to this collection are the 1879, 1880 and the 1881 coins which start at values of $250 in good condition and escalate into the $500 range for extra fine.

Pictured above is an 1877 nickel

It appears that there are very few error coins in this series but it does not mean that one will appear in the future.

The Liberty Head Nickel 1883-1913

The metal content of the nickel remained unchanged with the mintage of the liberty head, just a total redesign of the coin to show liberty on the front of the coin and the famous "V" on the reverse. This coin fell in line with most of the coinage of the day that placed liberty on the front of coins. Many collectors refer to this nickel as the "V Nickel." The first mintage of the coin did not denote cents on the coin, which could have left the "V" open for interpretation. The mint quickly modified the design to include the word "cents" on the first year of issuance in 1883.

By the time the mint changed the design, the mintage of the 1883 coin with the word "cents" was outpaced the nickel minted without cents. Today the 1883 with "cents" rises in value significantly above the issuance without the word.

No mint errors are widely publicized in this series.

The rarest coin in the series is the 1913 "V" nickel, selling in excess of $4 million. The US Mint since regarded this coin as illegal since it was not an authorized mintage.

Pictured above is the rarest known nickel

The keys to this collection are the 1885 with a value over $275 in good condition and the 1912-S with a value of $75 in good condition excelling to over $500 in extra fine condition. Many of these coins in the middle MS grades sell for more than $10,000 each at auction. There are proof-coins minted that can bring over $10,000 at auction.

We found that a complete set of liberty nickels sold for $14,500 in MS64 condition at auction. This is a bargain for this set since individually purchased coins of the same grade would far exceed the $14,500.

The Buffalo Nickel 1913-1938

The design of the buffalo nickel ended the rein of liberty on US coinage for nickels. The nickel design featured an American Indian on the front of the coin and a buffalo on the reverse of the coin.

The inherent problem with the buffalo nickel design was that the date was the highest point on the obverse causing it to wear off completely in coins that would otherwise grade good or very good. On the reverse of the coin, the horn of the buffalo became the focal point for coin grading. A coin with no horn is in good condition. A coin graded in very good condition revealed a partial horn. A grade of fine would show ¾ of the horn. A grade of very fine would entail showing a full horn with wear at the point. A grade of extra fine would require that the horn be fully outline with moderate wear. The best know error coin in the buffalo nickel series is the three- legged buffalo dated 1937-D. This is a true error coin. Refurbishing the die used to produce the coin continued until the leg wore off the die. .

Pictured above is a 1937-D 3-legged buffalo

As the picture above reveals, part of the front leg of the buffalo was missing. An MS66 encapsulated coin can sell at auction for over $80,000. The average value for a 1937-D 3-leg buffalo in good condition is around $165. The price steadily rises until the value of the coin exceeds $400 in extra fine condition.

The mint produced two versions of the 1913 buffalo nickel intentionally. One version portrays the buffalo on a mound and the second version shows the buffalo on flat ground. Collectors refer to these coins as type 1 and type two versions with mintages from Philadelphia, Denver, and San Francisco. Both versions are easy to recognize since there is a distinct difference between the mound and flat ground issues.

Buffalo nickel type 2 flat ground.

A notable error coin minted in 1914 resulted from using dies dated 1913. The mint produced coins with the four over the three. In good condition, one of these coins is valued at $125 and in extra-fine the coin is valued at $875. Coins in the higher grades of MS can reach auction bids exceeding $5,000.

Another well-known buffalo nickel is the 1916 double die obverse error. In good condition, this coin is valued at $1,600 and in extra-fine this coin can sell for more than $12,000. In MS63 condition, this coin can sell for $80,000 or more.

A more common buffalo nickel error is the 1918-D over seven where the mint used a 1917 die and punched an eight into the die leaving some of the seven on the die.

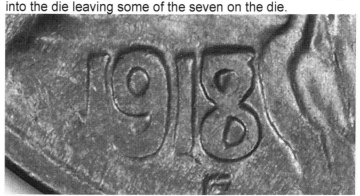

1918-8 over seven

The 1918/17 dated coins in MS condition of MS64 or better can sell in excess of $250,000.

In 1935, the mint produced a double die buffalo nickel valued at $35 in good condition and more than $2500 in MS60 condition.

As with many of the error coins in MS conditions, the prices realized are dependent upon the auction site and the number of bidders who are seeking that particular coin. This may explain the wide variances in at auction prices for some error coins.

1913 buffalo on mound (PCGS MS64, $115)

1913 buffalo on flat ground (PCGS MS64, $115)

1913-D buffalo on mound

1913-D buffalo on flat ground (NGC MS65, $126.50-$977) (high end is certified by CAC))

1913-S buffalo on mound (PCGS MS64, $230-$250)

1913-S buffalo on flat ground (PCGS MS64, $1,169)

1914 4 over 3 (PCGS MS64, $12,777) (PCGS MS65, $18,400)

1916 DDO (NGC Fine, $977-$4,800) (PCGS VF25, $5,885) (PCGS EF40/45, $17,825-$22,425) (NGC AU50, $1,725 under sold) (PCGS MS64, $184,000-$264,500)

1917 DDR (PCGS MS64, $10,925) 2015

1918 DDR (PCGS VG10, $235) 2015
1920 struck on a one-cent planchet (NGC AU55, $4,945)
1926-S (NGC MS65, $43,700)
1918-D 8 over 7 (ANACS/PCGS Good, $690/$977.50)
(PCGS VF30, $4,887-$6,612) (PCGS EF45, $4,887-$7,475)
(NGC AU53, $13,800)
(PCGS MS65, $155,000-$264,000)
1930 DDO (PCGS MS64, $165-$550) 2015
1930 DDR (PCGS AU50, $115) 2015
1930-S S over S (ANACS MS62, $431)
1934 DDO (ANACS AU50, $315) 2015
1935 DDR (NGC F12, $39) (PCGS VF20, $149.50) (PCGS
VF25, $276) (PCGS MS65, $25,300)
1936 DDO die 1(ANACS MS63, $110) 2015
1936-D three ½ legs (PCGS not graded damaged, $488.75)
1937-D three legged (NGC VF20, $603.75-$650) (NGC
EF45, $750- $776.25) (NGC AU55, $1000-$1,150) (PCGS
MS64, $8,050) (PCGS MS66, $86,250)
1938-D D over D (NGC AU58, $38) (PCGS MS66, $54-
$185)
1938-D D over S (NGC MS66, $95-$175)
1938-D D over S over mint-marked.

The Jefferson Nickel 1938-date

In 1938, the first Jefferson nickel minted in 1938 along with
the last issue of the Buffalo nickel. Since the Buffalo nickel
minting continued, the Jefferson 1938 series was limited in
production. This made the 1938-D and the 1938-S Jefferson
nickels semi-key coins to the collection. By the 1960's the
38-D and S coins were rare in circulation and could not be
easily located.

The keys to the Jefferson nickel collection are the 1939-D
and 1950-D coins but some of the other dates actually are
rarer and more valuable in the MS conditions.

The first error coin was the 1939 double die Jefferson nickel.
The values range from $26 in good condition to around $75
in extra fine condition. A coin in MS65 condition would sell at
auction between $1500 and $2000.

Many coin books do not list the Mint's die usage that created
some dates with the obverse of one date and the reverse of
another. In 1939, coins mintages included the reverse of
1940 with the obverse of 1939. Why the 1940 reverse
appeared on a 1939 coin resulted in using dies to reduce
costs. At auction, even with full steps in MS66 condition this

coin is valued at less than $50. Coins dated 1939 with the Denver mintmark appear with the reverse of a 1940.

There is some encapsulated Jefferson 1939-D coins with the obverse of 1939 and the reverse of 1938. These will sell at auction for less than $100 in MS condition. There are some 1939 double struck "Monticello" coins. These would sell for $5000 or more with full steps in higher MS grades.
The 1943 mintage contained some coins that used a 1942 die resulting in coins with three over two. The values range from $35 in good condition to over $90 in extra fine condition.
The pre-war 1942 D Jefferson nickel contained mintage with a D over horizontal D. The D mint- mark was located to right side on Monticello and the double D is clearly apparent. A full step double D coin can reach a value between $8,000 and $30,000 in mid-range MS grades.

Pictured above is 1942-D/D Jefferson nickel
There is some 1945 P double die reverse war nickels minted that year. The most significant sale price realized for this coin was just under $5000.
A double die 1946 appeared with a double D. There are samples   encapsulated and sold at auction bringing the same values as the 42 double D. The double D is the result of a re-punched die by a mint engraver.
In 1949, the Mint used the San Francisco dies modified to produce coins in Denver. This resulted in many D over S coins. A coin in MS66 with full steps can yield $8,000 or more at auction. A circulated coin might bring $25.
In 1954, the mint produced some Jefferson nickels with the S over D. A 1954 S over D in circulated condition holds a

value of $16 in extra fine condition with that price escalating to a few thousand for a coin in the middle MS grades.

In 1955, the mint produced Jefferson nickels with the D over the S. This coin retains a value close to the 1954 S over D error.

There are two versions of the proof Jefferson minted in 1979 and again in 1981. One version contained a normal mint marked S and the second version was struck with a closed S. Today, many of these coins' still remain in the original proof set enclosures.

Since 1981, it appears that the mint has done a good job of ensuring that no error coins result in any significant amount. As with all of these types of error coins, the value is what someone is willing to pay.

A coin collector might find some error nickels of interest on eBay.

Remember: Exercise care with coins listed on eBay that not encapsulated and presented as errors. Buyers using eBay to purchase error coins not encapsulated do risk the opinion of the seller.

Below is a listing of Jefferson nickel error coins that have sold at well-known and high-end auctions. Most of the valuable error coins in the Jefferson nickel series contain full step samples.

Jefferson Nickels

1938 DDO (PCGS MS64FS, $500) 2014

1938 D over D (PCGS MS65, $125) 2016

1939 DDO and DDR (ANACS MS 65, $58) 2015

1939 DDR (ANACS MS65, $58) 2015

1939 reverse of 1938 (PCGS PR68, $2,990- $9,775)

1939 reverse of 1938 DDR (ANACS AU58, $65) 2015

1939 reverse of 1940 (PCGS PR66 cameo, $2,875-$8,625)

1939 double Monticello (PCGS MS66 full steps, $1100-$6,900)

1939 DDO (ANACS, MS65, $58) 2014

1939-D reverse of 1938 (PCGS MS66, full steps, $4,715-$7,425)

1939-D reverse of 1938 DDO (PCGS MS67, $500) 2015

1939-D reverse of 1940 (PCGS MS66 full steps, $3,593)

1939-D (PCGS MS67, $500) 2015

1939-S reverse of 1938 (PCGS MS66 full steps, $8,050)

1939-S reverse of 1940 (PCGS MS66 full steps, $2,875)

1941 struck on a Lincoln cent (NGC VF20, $940) 2015

1941-S large S (PCGS MS65, $75) 2014
1942 type one DDO (PCGS MS65, $690) 2014
1942 DDO (NGC MS64, $92) 2015
1942-P (NGC MS66, $235) 2015
1942-D D over horizontal D (MS64 full steps, $32,200)
(PCGS MS65, $8,280- $12,650)
1940 reverse of 1938 (PCGS PR68, $28,750)
1943 P 3 over 2 (PCGS MS67 full steps, $2,530-$16,675)
1943 P DDO (ANACS F12, die 6, $9) (PCGS MS65, $635)
(PCGS MS66, $920) (PCGS MS67, $2,990-$11,500)
1944-P struck on copper nickel planchet (NGC VF30, $6900)
1945-P DDR (PCGS MS66, $2,760-$4887.50)
1946-D D over D (PCGS MS66 full steps, $3,600-$11,500)
1946-S DDO (PCGS MS65, $2,875)
1949-D D over S (PCGS MS65, $8,050)
1951 DDO (NGC PR67, $75-$200) 2014
1953 DDO (PCGS PR67, $90) 2014
1954-S S over D (PCGS MS66, $3,450)
1955-D D over S (PCGS MS66, $3,737)
1961 DDR (ANACS MS65 FS, $130) 2016
1971 proof missing S (PCGS PR69, $2,990-$4,485)
1977 struck on a 1976 cent (NGC MS64, $4600) 2015
1990-S DDO (NGC PR69, $525) 2014
1998 struck three times (NGC MS64, $950) 2014
2004-P double reverse (NGC, MS64 not sold)
2004-P peace metal DDO (NGC MS64, $50-$100) 2014

Chapter 8 – Half Dimes 1794-1873

It is ironic that the mint produced a ½ dime while nickels were minted starting in 1866. The half-dime series provides many coins with variations. The mint changed the half dime design several times to include the flowing hair design dated 1794 to 1795. The draped bust with a small eagle dated 1796 to 1797 was minted. The draped bust dime mintage included a large eagle dated 1800 through 1805, the liberty cap dime from 1829 through 1837, a seated liberty dime from 1837 through 1859, and a final design dated 1860 through 1873 with the addition of the United States of America on the obverse.

Pictured above is an 1800 ½ dime-Draped bust design

The dime above is an example of an 1800 ½ dime. Note the poorly stamped date of 1800 where the eight is oddly shaped.

In 1796 the mint produced a six over five ½ dime. Most coin guides will show this coin's value slightly more than a well struck 1796 coin. A five over six half dime in MS66 condition sold for more than $170,000 at auction. In 1796, the mint produced some variations, coins with 13 stars, 15 stars, and 16 stars. In addition, there were coins minted with the word "LIBEKTY". Coin guides may show many of the errors listed herein as approximately the same value in all grades. In 1800, the mint produced "LIBEKTY" error coins; however, these coins have no appreciable value verses coins with "LIBERTY".

In 1835, two types of dates came from minting process. The coins revealed both small and large dates. There is no significant value difference between the small and large dated coins.

In 1837, the mint produced large and small date coins. The small date 1837 is valued at 3 times that of the large date in

MS conditions. There were also coins with small dates and no stars and large dates with no stars minted in 1837.

In 1838, there were two versions, one with large stars and another with small stars. The small star version is valued at 2 times the large star coins in MS conditions.

In 1839, the New Orleans mint produced coins with a large O, and coins with a normal O. The large O is extremely rare.

Coins minted in 1840 from the New Orleans mint contained drapery and no drapery. Coins with no drapery can reach values at 10 times that of coins with drapery. The Philadelphia mint also produced the 1840 coins with drapery and no drapery. Both versions of the Philadelphia coins list as the same value in most coin guides.

In 1861, the mint used dies from 1860 minting coins with the one over zero. In MS65, these coins can have a value over $3500. In good condition, this coin is valued at $21 and rises to $220 in extra fine.

In 1872, the San Francisco mint produced one version of the coin with the S in the wreath and another version with the S below the wreath.

The poorly minted ½ dime is most likely subject to many flaws and perhaps some unknown errors. A collector should be aware of the numerous numbers of these coins with cleaning, plugs, and alterations. Many samples have bent or clips around the coin but they may still considered valuable because of the limited issues.

Chapter 9– Dimes
1796-1891

With all the versions and errors minted in this series, there are only a few years of no error or no version coins.

The first dime appeared in 1796. The second year of mintage in 1797 yielded two versions of the coin. One version was with 13 stars and the second version was with 16 stars. A search of US statehood attainment revealed that at the time of the minting of this coin in 1796 there were actually 16 states. Perhaps this is why the Mint decided to produce 16 star coins. Vermont attained statehood in 1791, Kentucky in 1792, and Tennessee in 1796 making 16 states in all.

In 1798, the mint produced coins with 1797 dies. These coins have errors in both productions of the 13 star and 16 star versions. In addition, the mint produced a small date and a large date 1798 coin. Why the mint produced coins with 13 stars in 1797 is anyone's guess since there were 16 states at the time. Perhaps the mint wanted to get more use out of the older dies that were expensive to make back in the 1700's.

It appears that the mint could not decide to make coins with 13, 14 or 16 stars because in 1804 more coin variation became available. The 1804 series resulted in coins produced with 13 stars and 14 stars. The 14 star reverse is more valuable than the 13 star versions. No coin mintage in 1804 contains 16 stars.

In 1805, die variations on the reverse of the coin produced coins with four and five berries. The coins with five berries are more valuable in all conditions.

Some coins dated 1811 reveal minting from dies of 1809 yielding coins with 11 over nine. There are no coins that are simply dated 1811 since all issues show the 11 over nine date.

Three coin versions appeared from mintage in 1814. One version is a large date, another is a small date, and a third version is STATES OF AMERICA with no spaces between the letters. The small dated coins are the most valuable followed by the large date, then the closed letters in the wording "States of America."

In 1820, two versions from the O mint produced a small o and a large O coin. The small o coin is the more valuable of the two versions. The 1821 coins yielded two versions, the small o and the larger O versions. The small o version is the more valuable of the two.

In 1823, the mint produced all of the coins with 1822 dies making a 23 over 22. Two other versions were minted, one with a small "e" and another with a large "E". The large "E" version is the more valuable coin.

In 1824, the mint again used the 1822 dies and modified them for 1824. All of these coins show a 24 over the 22. There were also two versions, one version of the coin with a large "E" and another with a small "e".

The 1828 series of coins have three versions. One version with a large date, another with a small date, and a third version with a small $.10 on the reverse of the coin. The large date version is the most valuable.

In 1829, three versions of the coin became part of the total mintage. One version with a small $.10, one version with a large $.10, and another version with a medium date are available.

The 1830, coins minted resulted with three versions. One version of the 1830 minted with a large $.10 and another with a small $.10 on the reverse of the coins. A die error resulted in producing the coin using modified 1829 dies yielding 30 over 29 coins. The large $.10 is the most valuable.

In 1834, the mint produced coins with a small four and a large four. Both of these coins are selling for approximately the same price.

The scarcity of the early dimes 1796 through 1830 is evident by the lack of availability of them at auctions. Any of these dates in XF or better in MS conditions will sell between $3,000 and several hundred thousand in the highest MS conditions available. Collectors are even willing to pay for coins with scratches, dents, nicks and other damage in grades of fine or better. Some dates in fair condition can bring $100 or more at auction.

Many of these coins appear altered and cleaned and buyers should be extremely careful when purchasing or bidding on any of these early dimes.

1838 small stars DDR (ANACS XF45, $220) 2015
1838 large stars DDR (ANACS XF40, $150) 2015
1855 arrows DDO (NGC MS63, $575) 2015
1871 DDO (ANACS PR63, $285) 2015

1876 DDO (PCGS VF30, $173) 2015
1876 DDR (PCGS MS62, $410) 2015
1876-CC DDO (NGC XF45, $160) 2015
1877-CC DDR (PCGS XF45 cleaned, $84) 2015
1889 DDR (PCGS VF30, $72) 2015

Dimes – Barber 1892 to 1916

With the production of the Barber dime, the mint was able to gain some perfection in the minting process. More attention to die use and maintaining the dies and hubs led to less error coins and variations.

In 1893, the mint produced an error coin by using dies of the 1892 version. There were a number of three over two mint errors placed into circulation. These coins sell for $4000 or more in the mid-MS range.

The mint produced a variation in 1905 at the New Orleans mint by issuing a micro O and a normal O coin. The micro O, the more valuable of the two coins, can sell from $25 in good to over $150 in extra fine condition.

This set is very accessible by collectors with the exception of a few coins with low mintages. The key coins to this set are the 1892-S, 1893-O, 1894-O, 1894-S (extremely rare), 1895, 1895-O, 1895-S, 1896-O, 1896-S, 1901-S, and the 1903-S. Note that the 1894-S has sold at auction for more than $1 million dollars in proof condition.

Pictured above is an 1803 Barber dime

Dimes – Mercury 1916 to 1945

The most revered and widely collected US dime is the Mercury dime. Many Mercury dimes are available in all grades for the collector. There is no shortage of any date including the 1916-D Mercury dime. If the collector has the funds a 1916-D in most any condition can be procured readily from a coin dealer or at an on line auction site. A check of eBay shows that there is always a listing for a 1916-D Mercury dime on the site.

In 1942, the mint produced a couple of error coins. The 1942 Denver minted dime can be found with an over date from 1941 showing a two over the one. In addition, the Philadelphia mint produced coins with a partial 42 over 41. Dimes in MS66 condition with this error have sold for as much as $70,000 at auction.

The mint produced two types of 1945-S coins, one with a normal S and another with a smaller S noted as the micro S. The micro s is the more valuable of the two variations; however, the micro S is not of any significant value in conditions less than mint state. These coins are always available on eBay. A high-grade sample of a 1916-D Mercury dime would appear be the highest selling coin at auction; however, research has revealed that a 1919-D MS66 full band PCGS coin sold for $218,500 versus a 1916-D higher graded sample in MS67 condition graded by PCGS that sold for $195,500.

Pictured above is a 1919-D Mercury dime

Mercury Dime Errors
1928-S DDO (PCGS MS65, $1265) 2015
1931-D DDO (ANACS AU55, $67) 2015
1931-S DDO (PCGS MS62, $115) 2015
1936 DDO (PCGS MS62, $65) 2015
1937 DDO (ANACS MS64 FB, $40) 2015
1937-S DDO (NGC MS68, $472) 2015
1940-S DDO (ANACS MS65, $50) 2015
1942 over 1 (PCGS VF30, $176-$922) (PCGS EF45, $322-$1250) (PCGS MS65, $9,775-$20,000) (PCGS MS66 full bands, $20,700- $71,875)
1942/1 D/D (ANACS AU55, $633) 2015

Dimes – Roosevelt 1946-
The Roosevelt dime mintage began in 1946 replacing the Mercury dime. Until 1965, all Roosevelt dimes were 90 percent silver and 10 percent copper. The vast majority of

Roosevelt dimes minted before 1965 disappeared from circulation for the silver content.

Most silver Roosevelt dimes are in conditions above very good because of the removal from circulation when the price of silver escalated in the early 1970's. It is relatively easy to obtain a brilliant uncirculated collection of Roosevelt dimes at a reasonable cost.

The perfection of the Mint's processes has restricted the error coins to a few dates in the Roosevelt dime series. A well know mint error occurred in 1950 with an S over mint-mark of a D. The range of value for this coin in mint state MS66 is between $200 and $300.

The next popular error is the 1960 double die proof dime with a range of $155 in PR65 to a higher range of $529 in conditions of PR68.

In 1963, the mint produced double die reverses on the Roosevelt dime that command auction values between $200 in conditions of PR65 to a top price of $700 in PR68. There are examples of 1964-D DDO Roosevelt dimes classified as MS65 that have sold at auction between $800 and $1840.

The mint produced a proof error in 1968 leaving the S off some of the coins in the proof sets. The 1968 no S proof coin is the most valuable error coin in the Roosevelt proof dime series ranging in value from $6,000 to $48,000.

In 1970, the mint produced proof sets with the S missing on some of the Roosevelt dimes in the sets. The 1970 no coins range in value from $285 to over $6,000 on proof condition. There two types of 1979-S proof dimes, a type1 and a type 2. The type one coins has a filled S and the other has a clear S. In 1981, there were two proof mint variations. Neither of these coins retains any significant value. As with the 1979-S proof coins, the 1981-S coins were minted with a filled S.

In 1983, the mint produced proof sets missing the S mint-mark on some coins. The 1983 no S coins are valued from $550 to near $2,000.

In 1982, there were numerous coins located without the P mint- mark. The large number of these coins minted has resulted in a small premium even in the highest MS conditions. This coin error sells for a reasonable price in various MS conditions ranging from values of $95 to over $2,000.

62

Pictured above is a 1951 Roosevelt dime

To date the Roosevelt dime is the only circulating coin to escape design modifications by the mint. Even when most of the U.S. coinage design changed in 1976 to display 1776-1976 as the date, the dime remained unchanged. The only change made to the coin was to add a P in 1980 to the obverse of the coin.

Listed below, are the major Roosevelt dime errors from completed auctions:

1941-D DDO (PCGS MS65 FB, $220) 2015
1946 D D over D (PCGS MS66, $50) 2016
1946 DDO (PCGS MS65, $40) 2014
1946 DDR (PCGS MS65, $40) 2016
1946 DDO and DDR (ANACS MS62, $35) 2016
1946-S DDO (PCGS MS66, $23) 2014
1946-S DDR (ANACS MS65, $70) 2015
1946-S/S DDR (ANACS AU53, $104) 2015
1946-S/S/S DDR (NGC MS66, $90) 2015
1946-S/S/S/S DDR (NGC MS65, $40) 2016
1947- S S over S (PCGS MS66, $50) 2016
1947-D DDO (PCGS MS65, $60) 2016
1947-S DDR (NGC MS67, $140) 2015
1947-S S over D (PCGS MS66, $50) 2016
1948-S S over S (PCGS MS66, $50) 2016
1950-D DDR die 1 (ANACS MS64, $23) 2016
1950-S S over D (PCGS MS66, $200-$300)
1951-S S over S (PCGS MS66, $50) 2016
1952-S S over S (PCGS MS66, $50) 2016
1953-D D over horizontal D (PCGS MS66, $50) 2016
1954 DDR (PCGS MS65, $80) 2016
1954-S S over S (PCGS MS65, $40) 2016
1959-D inverted D (PCGS MS66, $100) 2016
1959-D D over D (PCGS MS64, $35) 2016

1960 DDO (PCGS PR65 full bands $155-$275) (NGC MS66 full bands, $230) (PCGS PR67DCAM, $345-$529)
1960 DDR (NGC PR64, $52) 2015
1961-D DDR (PCGS MS66, $50) 2016
1962-D D over horizontal D (PCGS MS66, $150) 2016
1963 DDR proof (PCGS PR 65, $200) (PCGS PR 66, $155) (PCGS PR
67, $120) (PCGS PR 68, $375-$700)
1963 DDO (ANACS MS64, $40) 2015
1964 pointed 9 (PCGS MS66, $20) 2016
1964 blunt 9 (PCGS MS66, $20) 2016
1964-D DDO (PCGS MS65, $800-$1,840)
1964-D blunt 9 (PCGS MS66, $20) 2016
1964-D DDR (PCGS AU55, $57) 2015
1968 DDO (PCGS MS65, $30) 2016
1968 proof no S (PCGS PR68, $6,037-$48,875)
1968-S DDO (NGC PR67 $50) (NGC PR68, $185) 2015
1968-S DDR (ANACS PR64, $27) 2015
1969 reverse of 1968 (PCGS MS65, $50) 2016
1969-D over D (PCGS MS65, $30) 2014
1970 reverse of 1968 (PCGS MS66, $50) 2016
1970 proof no S (PR67, $285-$750) (PR68, $600-$6,037)
1970-D DDR (ANACS MS65, $55) 2015
1970-D reverse of 1968 (PCGS MS66, $50) 2016
1982 no P (PCGS MS64, $95-$120) (PCGS MS65, $145-$375) (PCGS MS66, $240-$345) (PCGS MS67, $290-$800) (PCGS MS68, $1,782- $2,185)
1983 proof no S (PCGS PR68, $550-$1,955) (PCGS PR69, $800-$1,955)
1999 Triple bonded multiple struck (NGC MS64, $3000) 2016

Above is a triple bond with multiple strikes

Chapter 10 – Twenty Cent 1875-1878

Perhaps a mint experiment that that never gained popularity; was the twenty cent piece which only lasted four years. The mint produced two years fro circulation, the 1875 and the 1876. The 1877 and 1878 mintages were available in proof only. The 1876CC coin is very rare and can bring a value of several hundred thousand at auction.

The 1877 and 1878 mintages are 510 and 600 pieces respectively. These are so rare that it has been difficult to locate any that have recently sold at auction.

1875-S Doubled "$" mintmark (NGC MS65, $3220) 2015

Chapter 11– Quarters 1796-date
1796-1807 Draped Bust

There are mint errors in the 1806 mintage with the six over the five. Most coin guides will show no significant value between the normal coin mintage and the error mintage. This coin ranges in value from $200 in good condition to over $1000 in extra fine condition. At auction, an MS64 quarter sold for over $65000.

1815-1838 Liberty Cap

There were no quarters minted from 1808 through 1814. The mint changed the design of the quarter in 1815 from the flowing hair design to the liberty cap design.

Pictured above is an 1822 Liberty cap quarter

In 1818, a number of coins minted using the 1815 dies produced quarters with eight over five. The significance in value between the non-error and the error mintage confined to the MS graded coins. The circulated value range for this coin is $60 in good to $300 in very fine condition.

Two dies, one with a large 9 and one with a small 9 produced quarters in 1819. Both of these coins share the same value. Values range from $60 in good to over $300 in very fine condition.

In 1820, the New Orleans mint produced small o and large O quarters for circulation. The small o coin is of more value in

MS conditions. Values range from $60 in good condition to over $300 in very fine.

In 1822, the mint modified a die with $.50c and used this die by attempting to change the $.50c to $.25c. The result was mintage with $.25 over $.50. This error coin realizes a value of $1200 in good to over $5000 in very fine condition. The coin error is worth a substantial amount of money in MS conditions. A recent auction result rendered over $195,000 for an MS66 error coin.

In 1823, the mint used dies from 1822 resulting in coins stamped with the three over the two. This is an unusual coin since there are no known examples of 1823 coins not stamped over 1822. In very fine condition, this coin has a value well over $25,000.

Not mentioned in most coin guides is the 1824 over 1823 quarter. At auction, one MS64 encapsulated coin sold for over $160,000.

In 1827, the mint produced re-strike proof coins using an 1823 die. These coins in proof condition can bring over $100,000 at auction. In 1828, the mint produced coins with $.25c over $.50c quarters. These coins are valued up to four times as much as the non-error version. This mint error has a value range of $150 in good condition to 800 in very fine. The last well- known mint variety in this series was the production of two variations of the 1831 quarter. The 1831 coins revealed a small letter version and a large letter version. Both of these coins are of equal value.

1838-1865 Seated liberty

The seated liberty type quarter replaced the liberty cap design in 1838 with both types minted in 1838.

Pictured above is an 1838 Seated Liberty Quarter

The 1840-O seated quarter editions yielded one with drapery and one without drapery. There is no significant value difference in grades from good through extra fine.

In 1842 there were large and small date mintages produced by the New Orleans mint. The small dated version is the rarer of the two with values ranging from $300 to over $2000 in extra fine condition.

In 1843, there were large and small dated coins minted from the New Orleans mint. Both of these coins are valued the same.

In 1853, the mint issued some 1853 quarters resulting in error coins with a three over four. One variation resulted in the 1853 coinage with the coin produced over 52 with "no arrows."

In 1854, coins produced at New Orleans came with a large O and a normal O. The large O is the most valuable at 6 times the value of a normal O coin.

The 1856 mintage from the San Francisco mint rendered coins with an S over S. A coin in extra fine is valued at $640.

There is only one known minted coin dated 1866. Since there is only one and it has not been at auction recently it would be impossible to place a value on this coin.

1866-1891 Seated liberty
The mint changed the seated liberty coin in 1866 by adding a motto above the eagle "In God We Trust."

There were three versions of the 1873 coins. Coins without the arrows, mintage with an open three and other coins with a closed three. The closed three version of the coin is the most valuable of the mintages with a value of 5 times that of the other 1873 dates.

The Carson City mint issued coins with arrows and no arrows in 1873. The no arrow mintage is extremely rare and this coin should bring values in excess of $250,000 in mint state condition. In 1875, the mint permanently removed the arrows from the coin.

The 1877 San Francisco mint issued coins with a normal S and a horizontal S. The horizontal S is valued at 4 times that of the regular S.

1841-O DDO (ANACS AU58 details, $235) 2015
1844 DDO (ANACS AU50, $525) 2015
1847 DDO (ANACS VF20, $30) 2015
1847 DDR (ANACS XF40, $110) 2015

1892-1916 Barber Quarter

This series of quarters is very affordable for most dates in all grades from good through extra fine enabling a collector to locate most dates.

The rarest coins in this set are the 1896-S and the 1901-S mintages. The 1901-S escalates in value from $4,000 in good to over $10,000 in extra fine. At auction one 1901-S Barber quarter in about good condition sold for close to $3,000.

There may be error coins, however, none could be located for this book and none listed in any major coin guides or online sites.

Pictured above is a 1901 Barber quarter

Most Barber quarters in grades of MS65 or higher can bring over $2500 at auction.

1892 DDR (ANACS MS62, $255) 2015
1892-O DDO (NGC AU58, $285) 2015

1916-1930 Standing Liberty Quarter

The mint overlapped production of the standing liberty quarter with the last year of mintage for the Barber quarter. This made the 1916 standing liberty quarter as the most valuable coin in the collection with values starting at $1,500 in good and over $5,000 in extra fine.

Two variations of the 1916 coin were part of the mintage in Philadelphia, San Francisco, and Denver with coins minted with no stars and with stars under the eagle. The version with stars continued from 1917 through the end of the collection in 1930.

In 1918, the San Francisco mint issued with dates resulting in coins with the eight over a seven. This error is highly valued with values ranging from $950 in good to $5,000 in extra fine. At auction, an MS64 encapsulated coin sold for over $145,000.

Pictured above is a 1918/7 standing liberty quarter

1918 over 7 (PCGS MS64, $25,150-$149,500) (PCGS MS65, $46,000-$109,500) (NGC MS66, $97,750)

1932- Date Washington Quarters

The transformation of all mint issues with former Presidents on the major circulating coins continued with placing George Washington on the quarter replacing the liberty quarter.

There are many DDO Washington quarter errors with a wide range of values based upon the mintage, demand, and the condition.

The 1934 mintage resulted in double die issues. The double die is on the obverse of the coin as shown below. Again, keep in mind that all authentic double dies have a very clear doubling of letters and numbers, not to be confused with machine doubling. A 1934 MS66 DDO can bring over $9,500 at auction.

Above is a 1937 double die obverse with a doubling of the words "IN GOD WE TRUST." The defined doubling is not as robust in this design as in some other mint doubling errors but it is an authentic DDO coin.

Washington Quarter Errors

1932 DDO (ANACS MS62, $125-$235) 2014

1934 DDO (ANACS VG10, $46) (ANACS AU50, $175-$315) (PCGS MS63, $3,737-$4,300) (PCGS MS64, $3,200-$3,500) (PCGS MS65, $3,700-$6,600) (PCGS MS66, $4,887- $9,500)

1934 DDO die 1 (ANACS F12, $33) 2015

1934 DDR (ANACS VG10, $46)

1936 DDO (NGC G, $16) (ANACS AU58, $100)

1937 DDO (ANACS, F12, $322) (ANACS MS63, $3,725-$6,325) (PCGS MS64, $4,300- $14,950) (PCGS MS66, $19,550)

1937-D DDO (ANACS MS65, $98-$115) 2015

1937-S DDO (ANACS MS64, $271) (PCGS MS67, $2420) 2014

1938 DDO (PCGS AU58, $175) 2015

1939 DDO die 1 (ANACS MS63, $92) 2015

1939 DDO die 3 (ANACS MS64, $46) 2014

1939-D DDO (ANACS MS64, $37) 2015

1939-S DDO (ANACS MS63, $92) (ANACS MS64, $196) (PCGS MS66, $415) 2014

1940-D DDO (ANACS MS63, $145)

1940 D over D (ANACS MS63, $155) 2016

1940-S DDO (ANACS MS64, $42-$60) 2014

1940-S DDO and DDR (ANACS MS64, $42) 2014

1940-S over S DDO (ANACS MS63, $92) 2015

1941 DDO (NGC/PCGS MS66, $75-$207)

1941 DDR (ANACS AU55, $20) (ANACS MS63, $50) 2014
1941-D DDR (PCGS MS65, $223) 2014
1942 DDO (ANACS MS64, $25) 2016
1942 DDR (ANACS MS62, $35-$50) 2015
1942-D DDO (ANACS F12, $100) (ANACS VF35, $175-
$345) (ANACS AU50, $750-$1600) (PCGS MS63, $3,450)
(PCGS MS64, $5,175) (PCGS MS66, $4,300)
1943 DDO (ANACS MS63, $45-$100) (ANACS MS65, $275)
1943-D DDO (ANACS XF45, $21) (ANACS MS64, $173)
2014
1943-S DDO (ANACS AU55, $400) (PCGS MS64, $1,550)
(PCGS MS65, $3,400-$9,500) (PCGS MS66, $6,325-
$9,500)
1944 DDO (ANACS MS64, $70) 2015
1944-D DDO (PCGS MS63, $31-$55) 2014
1944-S DDO (ANACS MS63, $25) (PCGS MS67, $700)
1945 DDO die 1 (ANACS XF45, $24-$50) 2015
1945 DDO die 2(NGC MS66, $207) (ANACS MS66, $98)
1945 DDO die 5 (ANACS MS64, $21) 2015
1945-D DDO (ANACS MS63, $70-$100) 2015
1946-D (ANACS MS65, $35) 2015
1946-D D over S (ANACS MS64, $46)
1947-S over S (ANACS MS64, $50-$100) 2015
1949-D DDO (ANACS MS64, $30-$100) 2015
1950 DDR (ANACS MS65, $21-$30) (PCGS MS66, $115)
1950-D DDR (NGC MS63, $58) 2015
1950-D D over D (ANACS MS63, $62) 2015
1950-D D over S (ANACS VG10, $23) (PCGS F12, $47)
(NGC VF30, $48) (PCGS EF45, $126-$138) (ANACS MS63,
$62)
(NGC MS64, $2,358) (PCGS MS65, $4,025-$7,500) (PCGS
MS66, $3,737-$23,000) (NGC MS67, $4,000)
1950-S S over D (ANACS F15, $39) (PCGS VF30, $72.45-
$115) (ANACS EF45, $143.75) (NGC/PCGS MS65, $550-
$2,875) (PCGS MS66, $495-$4,255)
(NGC MS67, $3,600-$3,737)
1950-S S over S (ANACS MS65, $161)
1952 Reverse Brockage (NGC MS64, $4700) 2016
1953 DDO (PCGS PR65, $255) 2015
1953-D DDR (ANACS MS63, $30) 2015
1954 DDR (ANACS PR65, $30-$85) 2015
1956 DDR (ANACS MS65, $25-$50) 2015
1957 DDR (ANACS MS64, $18) 2015
1959 DDO (PCGS PR66, $60-$150) 2015

1959-D DDR (ANACS MS64, $14-$50) 2015
1960 DDR (PCGS PR65, $80.50) (PCGS PR66, $120.75)
1961 DDO (PCGS PR66, $70) 2015
1962 DDO die 1 (ANACS PR67, $23-$50) 2015
1962 DDO die 4 (ANACS MS65, $70) 2015
1962-D struck on quarter planchet (NGC MS62, $2000) 2016
1963 DDO (ANACS MS64, $30-$80) (PCGS MS66, $305)
1963 DDR (NGC MS64, $40-$80) (ANACS MS65, $50)
1964 DDO (PCGS MS63, $23-$55) 2014
1964-D DDR (PCGS MS62, $95) 2015
1964-D DDO (PCGS MS62, $25-$50) 2015
1965 struck on silver planchet (PCGS AU58, $14,500) 2016
1965 DDO (PCGS AU55, $575) 2014
1966 DDR (PCGS XF45, $925) 2015
1967 DDO SMS (NGC MS67, $149.50-$230)
1967 DDR (ANACS MS66, $20-$50) 2015
1968-D DDR (PCGS MS64, $375) 2014
1968-S DDO (PCGS PR66, $374) 2014
1968-S DDR (PCGS PR66, $196) 2015
1969-D D over D (PCGS MS65, $25-$50) 2016
1969-S DDO (PCGS PR65, $300) 2015
1970-D DDO (PCGS MS65, $250-$300) 2014
1970-D DDR (PCGS MS65, $242) 2015
1971 DDR (PCGS AU58, $1380) 2014
1971-D DDR (PCGS XF40, $1100) 2015
1972 DDO (ANACS, MS60, $31)
1973 struck on cent planchet (NGC MS65, $1400) 2016
1976-D DDO (PCGS AU58, $690) 2014
1990-S DDO (PCGS MS66, $350) 2016
State Quarter
1999-P CT – triple struck (ANACS MS63, $605) 2014
1999-P PA – struck on experimental planchet – (PCGS MS66, $6325) 2014
1999-P 170 degree rotation (PCGS MS62, $300) 2014
1999-D DE – clad layer missing (PCGS MS63, $350) 2014
1999-D DE struck on nickel planchet (PCGS MS64, $412) 2016
2000-P MA – clad layer missing (PCGS MS64, $368) 2014
2000-P MD – struck on 5C (NGC MS67, $1495) 2014
2001-P NY – double struck (PCGS MS66, $432) 2014
2001-D VT – clad layer missing (PCGS MS64, $238)
2004-D IA – clad layer missing (PCGS MS63, $520) 2014
2004-P FL – struck on 5C (PCGS MS67, $1600) 2014
2004-D WI – extra leaf high (PCGS MS63, $175) 2014

2004-D WI – extra leaf low (PCGS MS63, $175) 2014
2005-P MN – Extra tree (PCGS MS65, $25-$89) 2014
2005-P MN – DDO (PCGS MS65, $150) 2014
2005-P MN – DDR (PCGS MS65, $150) 2014
2005-D MN – DDO (PCGS MS68, $90) 2016`

Chapter 12– Half Dollars 1794-date

The first half dollar issued by the mint went into circulation in 1794. Many mint designs have followed since the first half dollar mintage.

Flowing Hair

The flowing hair design of 1794 and 1795 are rare coins since the mintage of the 1974 was 5,300 and the mintage for the 1795 was around 13,000.

In 1795, the mint issued three variations of the coin. The variations resulted in one design with two leaves on the reverse, one with a re-cut date, and one with three leaves under each wing.

Pictured above is a 1975 flowing hair design

1796-97 Small eagle half

Two designs of the 1796 half were issues, one design with 15 stars and the other with 16 stars. Some of these coins can sell for $50,000 or more in very fine condition.

Pictured above is a small eagle 1796

1801-07 Draped Bust

Two variations were minted in 1803, one with a small three and another with a large three. Both coin versions command the same price at auction.

In 1805, the mint produced coins with the five over four. These coins rise significantly in value in grades of extra fine and un-circulated.

In 1806, coins with the six over five and with an inverted six over six came from the mint. The mint also produced coins with a knobbed six with large stars and a knobbed six stem not through the claw of the eagle. The latter is extremely rare.

1807-36 Turban Head

This series of half dollar will yield many types of variations. The 1807 design yielded three variations, one with small stars, one with large stars, and $.50 over $.20 on the reverse of the coin.

In 1808, there was a mint production of eight over seven coins. Coins without the error are actually more valuable in the higher grades.

The mintage of 1812 produced halves with 12 over 11. This half gains significantly in value in MS conditions.

In 1814, the mint made all of its coins with a 14 over 13. The 1815 mintage was made entirely of 15 over 12.

The series has many over dated coins:

The 1817 mintage yielded coins with 17 over 13.

1817 over 4

1818 over 7

1819 over 18 with a large 9

1820 over 19

1822 over 21

1824 over 21 with other over dates

1827 over 6 and a curled 2

1829 over 27

The 1823 half-dollar produced two types of three on the coin; one considered a normal three and the other that is distinctly different.

In 1830, there were two types of zeros in the date, a small zero and a large zero.

In 1832, there were two variations of the lettering, small and large. Both coin mintages are valued the same.

In 1836, the mint produced a variation with a lettered edge 50 over 00.

Pictured above is an 1817 with the 7 over 4

1836-39 Turban Head / Capped Bust / Reed Edge
No significant variations during this mintage found by the writer.

Pictured above is an 1837 Turban head half-dollar

1839- 1866 Liberty Seated
The 1839 mintage produced coins with drapery from the elbow and no drapery from the elbow. The no drapery coin is more valuable of the two, especially in MS condition.

The 1840 coins come with small letters and large letters. The large lettered coin is the more valuable of the two.

The New Orleans mint along with the Philadelphia mint produced large and small dated coins. The small date O is rare in any condition.

Some 1844 coins have double dates. These are extremely rare and can exceed $10,000 in MS conditions.

In 1846, there were some coins with six over horizontal six and these are rare in any condition.

Some 1847 coins have a seven over six. These are rare and valuable in any condition

In 1853, the mint produced coins with arrow and no arrows at the New Orleans mint. Only three of the no arrows coins reportedly exist to date

Pictured above is an 1846-seated half

1866- 1891 Liberty Seated
The 1873 mintage produced coins with no arrows and with arrows on the reverse of the coin from the Carson City mint, the San Francisco mint, and the Philadelphia mint.
Other than the arrow, no arrow variations, there were not any major recorded mint errors during this time- frame of 1866 through 1891.

Pictured above - 1874 CC seated half

1892- 1915 Barber half
The Barber half mintage is relatively free of pronounced error coins as recorded in major coin guides or on online sites.

Pictured above is a 1908 D Barber Half

1916-1947 Walking Liberty

In 1916, the mint- mark appeared on the obverse of the coin. In 1917, the mint- mark on the coin appeared on either the front or the reverse of the coins. Both D and S mint- marks appear on 1917 coins on either the obverse or the reverse of the coin. These are very strong-dated and mint marked coins, which provide collectors with ample stock from the lowest grades through extra fine condition.

The mint did not make half dollars in this series in 1922 and from 1924 through 1926 and again from 1930 through 1932. Only San Francisco minted Walking Liberty halves in 1923, 1927, 1928, and 1933. The Walking Liberty halves dated 16-S on the obverse and the 1921 and 1921-D dates are the keys to the collection.

The most common dates are in the 1940's and collectors should have no problem locating these dates in circulated condition.

Pictured above is a 1919D walking liberty half

Error coins

1921 double struck (ANACS MS61, $16,100)

1936 DDO (PCGS MS65, $320) 2016

1936-D DDO (PCGS MS66, $750) 2016

1939-S DDO (PCGS MS67, $1750) 2016

1942 DDO (ANACS AU55, $35) 2016

1942 DDR (ANACS MS62, $71) 2016

1942 struck on silver quarter planchet (PCGS MS65, $17,600) 2016

1942-D DDO (ANACS MS65, $140) 2016

1945 DDR (ANACS MS64, $95) 2016

1945 struck on dime planchet (NGC MS64, $42000) 2016

1946 DDR (PCGS MS66, $7,000) 2016

1946-S DDR (ANACS MS65, $225) 2016

1948-63 Ben Franklin

There are a few major error coins in the series that are widely noted. Some off mintages of a 1955 and 1956 coin appeared and collectors deemed it as the "bugs bunny" coin but most major coin guides do not list this coin as an error. Although there is not a lot of recognition, coin collectors do pay a premium for the Bugs Bunny half.

Pictured above is a 1950 Franklin half

1948-D DDR (PCGS MS66, $1,035)
1950 DDO (PCGS PR66, $390) 2015
1952 struck on quarter planchet (NGC AU58, $1400) 2016

Above is a 1952 Half struck on a quarter planchet.
1955 struck on 5 cent (NGC MS63, $3650) 2016

1956 DDO (ANACS MS64, $43) (PCGS PR65, $153)
(PCGS PR68, $575)
1955 Bugs Bunny (PCGS MS65, $200)
1956 Bug Bunny (PCGS MS66, $240)
1956 struck on quarter planchet (PCGS MS65, $1650) 2016
1956 DDO (PR67 Cameo, $280) 2016
1956 DDR (PCGS PR68, $2,990)
1959 DDR (NGC MS65, $80) 2016
1960 DDO (NGC PR66, $172.50) (PCGS PR67, $382)
1961 DDR minor (PCGS PR66, $36-$189.75)
1962 Struck on a quarter planchet (NGC MS63, $2000) 2015
1963-D struck on quarter planchet (NGC MS65, $5000) 2016

Kennedy Half 1964-
The Kennedy half- dollar was never common in circulation.
Some experts have interpreted the lack of usage as inability
to use the coin in vending machines, or being too heavy to
carry in pockets, and that the early mintages with hoarded by
people for nostalgic reasons.
Casinos used most of the Kennedy half mintage for the slot
machines before the use of paper payout forms. Millions of
Kennedy halves wore beyond recognition from use in slot
machines.

Kennedy half mintages:
The 1964 issues are silver and command this premium
Mintages from 1965 through 1969 contain 40 percent silver.
The 1970 issue coin comes in proof only.
Kennedy halves minted for circulation: 1971-1986
In 1987, Kennedy halves appeared in proof sets only.
In 2001 through 2004, the mint made all issues of the
Kennedy half for mint and proof sets.
The 2005 mintage is in circulation.
From 2006 to date all Kennedy half production continued for
proof sets. The mint has been offering rolls of Kennedy
halves for sale on their web site for a number of years. It is
possible that some of these rolled coins will reach circulation
in the future. There is only one mintage year of 90 percent
silver for the Kennedy half that occurred in 1964.

Kennedy half-dated 1964

Research has uncovered some Kennedy half errors as listed below:

1964 DDO (ANACS PR66, $10)

1964-D DDO (ANACS MS64, $21) 2016

1964-D Struck on a quarter planchet (NGC, Mint Error, $1750) 2016

1964-D Struck on nickel planchet (PCGS MS64, $3525) 2016

1965 DDR (PCGS MS65, $600) 2016

1966 DDO SMS (PCGS SP65, $20-$28) (PCGS SP66, $47-$89) (PCGS SP67, $56-$126) (PCGS MS67, $161)

1966 Doubled profile (NGC MS67, $48)

1966 DDO and DDR (ANACS MS66, $25)

1966 no "FG" (PCGS SMS MS64, $60) 2015

1966 struck on quarter planchet (NGC MS63, $882) 2016

1967 DDR (ANACS MS66, $27)

1968-S DDO (ANACS PR63, $10)

1968-S DDR (ANACS PR66, $9) (H, ANACS PR67, $16)

1969-S DDO and DDR (ANACS PR67, $16)

1971 DDO (PCGS MS65, $100)

1971-D DDO (PCGS MS63, $24)

1971-S DDO (PCGS PR66, $50)

1973-D DDO (PCGS MS65, $200)

1974-D DDO (ANACS AU55, $45) 2016

1776-1976 DDR proof (PCGS MS65, $500) 2016

1977-D struck on 40% silver planchet (NGC AU55, $4200)

1977-D DDO (PCGS MS65, $650)

1982-P no "FG" (PCGS MS63, $50) 2014

Chapter 13 – Dollars 1794-date
1794-95 Flowing Hair Design
The silver dollar mintage began in 1794 and much like the half dollar the first design last only two years. The rarity of the 1794 silver dollar could bring over $20,000 in circulated condition.
1795-1804 Draped Bust
The mint changed the design in 1795 and minted both versions of the flowing hair and the draped bust types. The mintage of 1796 produced two varieties of the coin, one with small letters and another with large letters. Coins of 1797 were produced with small letters, large letters, 9 stars left and 7 stars right with small and large letters; and coins with 10 stars left and 6 stars right.

During the early series the US Mint issued a well know error coin every year until last year of mintage until 1836 when the mint resumed production of the silver dollar.
1836-1839 Liberty Seated
Silver dollars minted during this time contained an eagle on the reverse of the coin. All three mintages of this coin are extremely valuable.
1840-1866 Liberty Seated No Motto
There are no well-known error coins during this span of silver dollars. The 1866 mintage was struck in proof only and there are very few known.

Pictured above is an 1859

1866-1873 Liberty Seated with motto

In 1866, the motto "In God We Trust" became part of the silver dollar design. There are no well-known error coins in this time- period. There was a mintage of the 1873 coin at the San Francisco mint; however, no one has yet to reveal a coin in a collection. No one knows what happened to the 1873-S coins and if someone were to locate this coin, it would bring millions.

1841-O DDO (ANACS AU58 details, $235) 2015
1844 DDO (ANACS AU50, $525) 2015
1847 DDO (ANACS VF20, $30) 2015
1847 DDR (ANACS XF40, $110) 2015
1876 DDR (ANACS AU details, $345) 2015
1877-S DDR (PCGS XF45, $259) 2015

1873-1885 Trade Dollars

The mint needed to produce a dollar coin that competed with
the European coins of the same denomination. Since the
European coins were larger, the US had issues trading with
the silver dollar. The mint produced the trade dollar with
more silver content. The coin is thicker than other silver
dollars of that time. Shortly after the mintage of this coin, the
US Treasury department made the coin illegal to use in
domestic trade, restricting the coins for use in international
transactions.

Pictured above is a typical US trade dollar

1878-1904 1921 Morgan Dollar

The mint returned to the regular production of the silver
dollar for domestic use in 1878 changing the design known
as the Morgan dollar. The Morgan dollar is most widely
collected because of the numbers of coins available to
collectors at a reasonable cost.

The very first mintage of 1878 contained one coin minted
with eight tail features and another with seven tail feathers.
Coins produced using the 1879 reverse design can be
located. There was also an error coin minted in 1878 with
the seven over the eight containing eight tail feathers.

Leroy C. Van Allen and A. George Mallis cataloged most of
the Morgan dollar variations and errors. Together the two
collectors designated the error classifications as VAM's.
Thousands of cataloged VAM coins are available to the
collector at reasonable prices. Many collectors are not
concerned with the VAM designation when putting together a

set of these silver dollars. The VAM designation will always be a part of the encapsulation services such as NGC and PCGS. . It is within the scope of this book to provide realized auction sales of some VAM coins so that the collector has a reference value

Pictured above is an 1889 Morgan dollar

1878 8 Tail Feathers – proof like (NGC MS61, $420) 2015
1878 8 Tail Feathers (PCGS MS62, $207)
1878 7 Tail Feathers reverse of 1878 VAM 121, VAM 31 (PCGS MS62, $195.50)
1878 7 Tail Feathers Tripled Eye VAM 166 (PCGS AU50, $2000) 2015
1878 Rev of 1879 (ANACS AU50, $40) 2015
1878 Triple Blossoms VAM 44 (PCGS MS61, $14,000)
1878 Triple Eyelid VAM 50 (NGC AU58, $176)
1878 Spiked Eye (PCGS Unc Details, $350)
1878 DDO 8TF (NGC MS62, $282) 2015
1878-CC Doubled Leaves (NGC AU5, $915) 2015
1878-S Doubled "RIB" (NGC MS63, $104) 2015
1880 80 over 79 VAM 8 (PCGS MS66, $517.50)
1880-O 80 over 79 (PCGS MS62, $431.50) (PCGS MS63, $488.75)
1880-O Hang Nail (ANACS AU58, $65)
1880-O DDO (PCGS VF20, $149.50)
1881 DDO (NGC MS64, $825) 2015
1881-O Double Ear VAM 27 (PCGS, AU53, $140)
1882-O O over O (PCGS MS63, $100) 2015
1882-O Over S (PCGS AU55, $235)
1882-O Over S Flush S VAM 3 (PCGS AU55, $235)
1883 Sextupled Stars VAM 10 (NGC XF45, $300)
1883-O Over O VAM 4 (PCGS MS63, $80)
1883-O Partial E Reverse (PCGS MS63, $75)
1884 Partial E Reverse (NGC MS62, $100)

1884 Large Dot VAM 3 (PCGS AU55, $75)
1884-O Misplaced 88 VAM 25 (NGC MS63, $85)
1884-O O over O Doubled Ear VAM 10 (NGC MS65, $138)
2015
1884-O DDO Eyelid (NGC MS64, $106)
1884-O over O (PCGS MS64, $126.50)
1886 Line in 6 VAM 1A (ANACS MS65, $130)
1886 DDR Arrows (NGC MS65, $141) 2015
1886 DDR (ANACS MS62, $57) 2015
1886 Doubled Arrows VAM 17 (ANACS MS64)
1886-O Rotated Dies (NCG AU50, $200)
1886-O Clashed E VAM 1A (NGC AU55, $200)
1886-O Over O VAM 7 (NGC AU55, $440)
1887 DDO VAM 5 (NGC MS64, $115) 2015
1887 Donkey Tail VAM 25A (NGC VF details, $65)
1887 Gator Eye DDO (NGC MS65, $177) 2015
1887 7 Over 6 VAM 2 (NGC AU58, $165)
1887-O Clash VAM 30A (NGC AU53, $95)
1887-O Doubled 1 VAM 2 (NGC MS61, $99) 2015
1887-O Doubled Stars VAM 5 (NGC MS62, $200)
1887-O DDO (NGC AU53, VAM 22A $115)
1887-S S over S (PCGS MS63, $253)
1888 DDO VAM 11 Doubled Ear (NGC MS63, $66) 2015
1888 DDR VAM 12A (NGC MS63, $94) 2015
1888 Doubled Ear VAM 11A (NGC MS63, $80)
1888-O Clashed E VAM 1A (NGC MS62, $175)
1888-O O over O DDR (NGC XF45, $374) 2015
1888-O Oval VAM 21 (NGC AU55, $110)
1888-O DDO (NGC EF45, $360)
1888-O DDO VAM 4 Hot Lips (NGC VG10, $69) 2015
1888-O DDR Arrows (NGC MS65, $500) 2015
1888-O Hot Lips VAM 4 (NGC F15, $85)
1888-O Hot Lips DDO VAM 4 (NGC XF45, $260)
1888-O Doubled Arrows VAM 9 (NGC MS63, $70)
1889 Bar Wing VAM 19A (NGC MS61, $85)
1889 Doubled Ear (NGC MS65, $329) 2015
1889-O Clashed E VAM 1A (NGC VF30, $200)
1889-O Micro O (PCGS VF30, $50) 2015
1890-O Doubled Ear and Leaves VAM 20 (NGC VF30,
$200)
1890-O Weak Comet VAM 10A (NGC MS62, $115)
1891 Doubled Ear (NGC MS63, $127) 2015
1891-O Weak Clashed E, VAM 3A (NGC XF45, $300)

1892-O DDO (PCGS XF40, $38) 2015
1896 DDO (NGC MS64, $135) 2015
1896 Misplaced Date VAM 19 (ANACS MS63, $60)
1896 8 In Denticle (PCGS MS63, $80)
1896-O Shifted Date VAM 19 (NGC AU details, $65)
1897 Doubled Stars VAM 8 (NGC MS62, $90)
1900 DDR (NGC MS64, $112) 2015
1900 Doubled Arrows (NGC MS63, $84) 2015
1900 Misplaced Date, Double Olives VAM 16 (NCG MS63, $110)
1900-O O over CC (PCGS MS64, $862.50)
1900-O Doubled Stars (PCGS MS65, $173) 2015
1901 DDR Shifted Eagle (PCGS XF40, $825) 2015
1904-O Fishhook VAM 4B (NGC MS62, $84)
1921-D Capped R VAM 1B (PCGS AU53)
1921-D Unicorn VAM 1N (NGC MS62)
1921-S Thorn Head VAM 1B-4 (NGC AU58, $200)
*note: there are thousands of VAM error coins available for Morgan dollars.

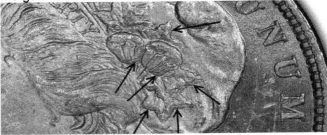

1878 Tripple Bloosoms

1921-1935 1964 Peace Dollar

The mint overlapped the design change from the Morgan dollar to the peace design in 1921.

Many coin publications purported that a 1964 peace dollar exists but no samples appear from known sources. The mint must have destroyed all of the mintage after deciding not to issue the coins. Will some of these coins show up like the 1913 V nickel in future? Only time will tell.

Pictured above is a 1934 peace dollar

1922 Extra Hair VAM 2C (ANACS MS63, $85)

1922 Triple Die Reverse VAM 5C (NGC MS62, $80)

1922 Line in Tiara VAM 1A (NGC MS62 1-A, $80)

1922 Hair Pin VAM 2F (NGC MS64, $75)

1922 Doubled Motto VAM 4 (NGC MS62, $90)

1922 Tripled Leaves & Eroded Face VAM 5C (NGC MS62, $70)

1922 Scar on Cheek VAM 5A2 (NGC AU58, $200)

1922 Doubled Leaves VAM 6 (NGC MS62, $55)

1922 Moustache VAM 12A (NGC MS62, $160)

1922-D DDO (ANACS AU50, $32) 2015

1922-D DDR (ANACS MS63, $547) 2015

1923 Chin Bar VAM 1F (PCGS MS62, $120) 2015

1923 DDO (NGC MS63, $127) 2015

1923 DDR Leaves (NGC MS62, $78) 2015

1923-D DDR Eagle (NGC AU55, $74) 2015

1925 DDR Shoulder (NGC MS64, $120) 2015

1925-S DDR Leaves (ANCAS AU58, $90) 2015

1926 DDR Leaves (ANACS MS64, $100) 2015

1927-D DDO Trust (PCGS MS65, $4025) 2015

1928-S DDO (ANACS AU55, $100) 2015

1928-S DDO motto (NGC MS63, $635) 2015

1928-S double die "IN GOD WE TRUST" (PCGS MS65, $13,800) Note that coins without the error in the same condition have sold for more at auction.

1934-D DDO Motto with large mint mark D (NGC MS63, $441) 2015

1934-D DDO small D mint mark (ANACS VF25, $130) 2015

1971-1978 Eisenhower Dollar

The US Mint decided to place a portrait of President Dwight Eisenhower on a coin after his death and to honor the World War II general. The reverse of the coin features the Apollo spacecraft in commemoration of space flight.

The coin was very unpopular from the start of the mintage since it was heavy and bulky to carry. Rarely did this coin circulate freely even though there was a continued mintage from 1971 through 1978. None of these coins carries any significant value. The mint did produce silver clad coins for mint and proof sets until 1978.

Pictured is a 1776-1976 Eisenhower dollar

Even for a short mintage, the recorded errors are few.

1971 DDO (ANACS MS64, $16) 2015
1971 DDR (ANACS AU55, $15) 2015
1971-S DDR (H, ANACS PR68, $20-$30)
1971-S DDO DDR (ANACS MS65, $35) 2015
1971-S DDR (ANACS PR66, $29) 2015
1972-D DDR (NGC MS66, $250) 2015
1973-S DDO (ANACS MS66, $56) 2015
1977-D struck on silver planchet (NGC MS63, $13,000) 2016

1979-1981 1999 Susan B Anthony

The mint determined that there was a need for a dollar coin to offset the cost of minting dollar bills and the mintage of the Susan B Anthony dollar began in 1979. After only three years of mintage, the mint found that stock plies of these coins remained in bank vaults and the mint ended production.

In 1979, the mint issued two variations of the 1979-P dated coins, one with a wide rim and the other a normal rim. The wide rim 1979-P is not off any significant value verses the standard rim coin. Neither the variation nor the non-variations are valued more than $1 in circulated condition. An MS64 1979-P wide-rim sample has a low value of $25 at auction.

No DDO, DDR or RPM coins could be located at auctions. After 18 years, the mint stamped out a 1999 Susan B coin when vending machines and tolls accepted the dollar coin.

The Susan B Anthony series lacks any major coins errors that could be located on major auction sites.

Susan B Anthony errors

No DDO or DDR coins located

1979-P wide rim (NCG MS64, $19-$31) (NCG MS65, $42-$44) (NCG MS66, $104-$128) (NCG MS67, $920-$977)

The wide rim and the normal rim coins sell at auction in the same range, making the wide rim version nothing significant.

No date – Struck on a brass cent (PCGS AU58, $3450) - 2015

1979-P struck on a quarter planchet (ANACS MS63, $690) 2015

1979-S struck on a cent planchet (PCGS MS64, $5400) 2015

1979-P struck on a quarter planchet (ANACS MS63, $690) 2015

1979-S struck on a cent planchet (PCGS MS64, $5400) 2015

Susan B Anthony minted on a brass planchet

2000- Sacagawea Dollar

The mint dropped the Susan B in favor of a golden colored dollar they for circulation. Unfortunately, this dollar coin has not added significantly to the circulated coin stock. The dollar mintage continued every year for proof sets and special rolled issues by the mint. Only the 2000, 2001, and the 2012 Sacagawea dollar production is for circulation.

The 2010 coin saw a change to the reverse of the coin and the movement of the date to the rolled edge of the coin. There has been a new design every year from 2010 through 2013.

Sacagawea dollars
2000-P struck on a Susan B planchet (PCGS MS66, $8050) 2015
2009 missing letter edging (PCGS MS66, $150) 2014

2007- Presidential dollars
The presidential commemorative dollar series began in 2007 with the issuance of George Washington. With the very first issuance of this series, a number of Washington Presidential dollars appeared without the edge lettering. At auction, a collector can obtain an encapsulated mint state 65 for less than $50. There are many error coins in this series with missing letter edging of a number of coins that can bring the collector some significant auction dollars. Values of some of the error coins can range from $35 to over $2,000 for coins graded in the highest mint state conditions. Take care when bidding on any of the coins missing edge lettering since it is

a relatively new find and there may be a tendency to over pay for a sample.

In Chapter 13, there is a listing of all of the coins sold at auction with the final auction prices to give the collector an idea of what the market values are currently.

Below is a listing of the most current Presidential coin errors and the prices paid at auctions.

Presidential Dollar Errors

2007 John Adams Double Edge Letters (NGC MS64, $35) (NGC MS65, $50) (NGC MS66, $241-$748) (PCGS MS67, $1,150)

2007 John Adams Missing Letter edge (ANACS MS65, $50)

2007 John Adams Rotated 85 degrees (PCGS MS64, $150) 2016

2007 John Adams Double Edge Lettering (PCGS Uncirculated, $150) 2016

2007 George Washington Missing Edge Lettering (NGC MS65, $30-$56) (NGC MS66, $36-127)

2007 Thomas Jefferson Missing Edge Letters (PCGS MS65, $50) (PCGS MS66, $546-$1,035) (PCGS MS67, $747.50-$1,495)

2007 James Madison Missing Edge Letters (NGC MS65, $50)

2007 James Madison –double edge lettering (PCGS MS65, $100) 2014

2007-S Thomas Jefferson Double Struck with Rotation (NGC PR69, $460)

2008 Andrew Jackson Missing Edge Letters (PCGS SP67, $153) 2016

2008 James Monroe Missing Edge Letters (PCGS SP66, $300) 2016

2008 John Quincy Adams Missing Edge Letters (PCGS SP66, $49) 2014

2008 Martin Van Buren Missing Edge Letters (NGC MS66, $460) (NGC MS67, $1,265) (NGC MS68, $1,840)

2009-D Zachary Taylor Missing Letter Edge (NGC MS66, $431.25)

2009 William Henry Harrison Missing Letter Edge (NGC MS66, $432) (NGC MS67, $575-$1,150) (NGC MS69, $1,955)

2009 James K Polk Missing Letter Edge (NGC MS65, $50)

2009 John Tyler Missing Letter Edge (NGC MS67, $503.70)

2009 Zackery Taylor Missing Letter Edge (NGC MS66, $150) 2016
2010 James Buchanan Missing Letter Edge (PCGS MS66, $170) 2016
2010 Millard Fillmore Missing Letter Edge (NGC MS66, $460)
2012 Cleveland Missing Letter Edge (PCGS MSMS64, $50)

Chapter 14 – Modern Day Coin Errors

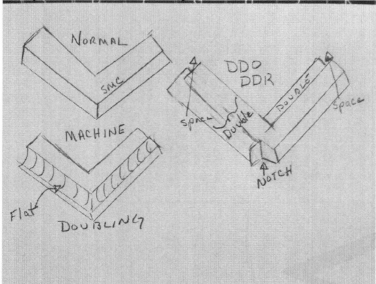

Above is the author's rendition of hub doubling and machine doubling on coins.
The normal lettering and dates shown above in the upper left. The machine doubling shown below and to the left reveals flat doubling. The drawing in the upper right shows notches and spaces with the doubling the same height as the normal letter and numbering.

The majority of encapsulated error coins are double die mintages with various degrees of doubling. The collector should be familiar with doubling by mint dies and machine doubling. Machine doubled coins do not command any additional value.

Above is a 1972-S machine double
Double Die Coins in Circulation

95

The 1972-S Lincoln cent photograph is an example of a machine doubled coin. A true double die will have an overlap of the letters or numbers with the height of the doubling the same. The example above is simply flashing around the numbers.

A 1972 Double Die Lincoln Cent

Above is a true double die cent. Note the doubling of the date is the same height in the numbers. All double dated coins have the same features as shown above.

Shown above is a 1959-D/D/D Lincoln cent
In the above photograph is a picture of a 1959 Lincoln cent with a triple D. Note the doubling all around the D.
1959-D triple D (ANACS MS63, $154) (PCGS MS65, $26-$184) (PCGS MS66, $30-$116)

A PCGS 1960-D large date D over D

Among the doubling errors for the 1960 coins, there is a 1960 large date D over D. Others include DDO's for both large and small dates.

1960 D over D small over large date (PCGS MS65, $205) 2014

A PCGS 1960 Lincoln cent small date over large.

Form this photograph clearly the small zero is over the large zero. There are also noticeable doublings over the nine and the six.

1960 DDO Small over Large date (PCGS PR65, $299) (PCGS PR66, $276) (NGC PR67, $385), (PCGS PR68, $4600)

1960 DDO Large over Small Date (PCGS PR67, $300-$400), (PCGS PR68, $603-$1,006), (PCGS PR69, $7475)

1960-D DDO Small over Large Date (PCGS MS65 red, $658) 2014

1960-D DDO Large over Small Date (NGC PR64, $109) (NGC PR65, $138-$219) (NGC PR66, $161-253) (NGC PR67, $253-483)

1960-D DDO Small over Large Date (PCGS PR66, $276) 2014

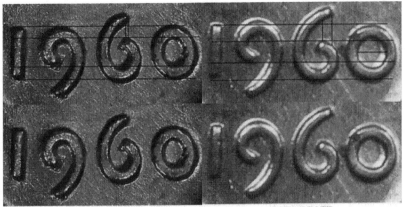

SMALL DATE   LARGE DATE

Above is a photograph of the comparison of the 1960 large and small dated coins.

A 1963-D DDO

Note in this coin the doubling of the D and a sharp doubling of the three.

1963-D DDO (PCGS MS64, $38) 2011

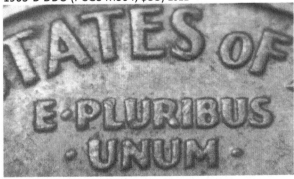

98

A 1964 double die reverse
Perhaps somewhat difficult to catch, there is doubling in the E.P.U and Sates.
1964 DDR (NGC MS62, $34)

Pictured above is a 1968-D over D Lincoln Cent
The D over D in the 1968 cent is clear enough to recognize without using a magnifying glass. As with most of the double mint marks the coin sells for a reasonable amount in high mint state grades.
1968-D over D (PCGS MS65, $165) 2014

1968-D double die reverse
The best way to detect this coin error is to inspect the FC on the reverse of the coin. The doubling is very clear.
1968-D DDR (PCGS MS64, $100-250) 2016

1969-S Double Die Lincoln cent

1969-S Lincoln cent double die
The two photographs above depict the famous and very valuable 1969-S double die Lincoln cent. Note the doubling of the lettering which is the same height through out. The date doubling results with the numbers the same height.

1964 DDO Lincoln cent

Above is a 1964 Lincoln cent with strong doubling of AM and ES. The doubling of letters shows the raised lettering a feature of true doubling.

Some double die cents classify as "minor" and there are those considered as "major" errors. The minor errors will command less in the market verses those like the 1969-S double die Lincoln cent the command thousands.

Pictured above is a 1980 double die

One of the most difficult double dies to detect in the Lincoln cent coinage. There is doubling in the 80 and in the motto.
1980 DDO (PCGS MS64, $160-$600) (PCGS MS65, $1750) 2016

A 1982 double die Lincoln cent

The doubling occurs in the letters shown above and in the ONE.
1982 DDO large date die 2 (ANACS MS65, $21)

A 1983 double die obverse cent

There are many variations to the 1983 double die cent including
DDR examples
1983 DDO (NGC MS64, $42-$70)

Above is a very distinct 1983 double die reverse
1983 DDR (PCGS MS64, $213) (NGC MS68, $3,220)

102

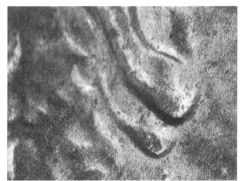
Double ear 1984 DDO
The 1984 Lincoln cent error is on Lincoln in the form of a double ear.
1984 DDO (ANACS MS62, $51) (PCGS MS65, $219) (PCGS MS66, $495) (PCGS MS67, $630-$805)

1995 Double Die
The 1995 double die Lincoln cent is affordable for less than $50 depending on the grade. High grades of mint state command prices in excess of $50. The doubling on this coin is in LIBERTY with the doubling very pronounced in the B E and R. This coin would be difficult to locate in circulation.
1995 DDO (PCGS MS67, $69-$74) (PCGS MS68, $79)

1995-D Lincoln cent double die

The picture above represents a 1995-D DDO type 3 die reveals a heavily pronounced doubling of the WE, GO in GOD, and RU in the motto.
1995-D DDO (PCGS MS64, $300-$800) (PCGS MS65, $550-$1100)

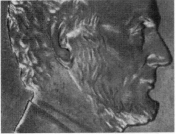
A 1997 double ear Lincoln cent

First discovered many experts refused to agree that it was a true doubling. This coin error is now widely accepted as a die error.
1997 double ear (PCGS MS65, $195.50)

A 2006 Lincoln cent double die.

The 2006 double die Lincoln cent shows doubling most pronounced in the motto.

Above is a 2006 double ear Lincoln cent

105

Lincoln cents 1909-1958
There are numerous Lincoln cent errors dated 1909 through 1958. Since these coins are not common in circulation because the "wheat back" hoarding, it is difficult to locate errors from pocket change. Below are a number of Lincoln cent error coins that are of prominence in the collecting community.

The 1909-S issues have mintages with a double S. These coins noted as S over horizontal S. Coins range in value with grading as follows: (ANACS VG10, $89) (NGC MS63, $299-$345) (NGC MS64, $518) (PCGS MS65, $1006) (PCGS MS66, $2,070)

Above is an example of a 1917 double die.
The doubling is in the We and TRUST in the motto.
1917 DDO (PCGS G04 $69) (PCGS F12 $144) (raw EF40, $978) (PCGS MS66, $25,300-$28,750)

Above is a 1922 no D Lincoln cent.
Some of these coins circulated for a length of time since there are coins available in all grades. The reason that rare Lincoln cents before 1940 are available in the lowest grades is that coin collecting did not catch fire until the first coin guides circulated in the mid-nineteen-forties
1922 no D or partial D (PCGS G6, $250) (ANACS VG8, $800) (PCGS AU55, $4113) (PCGS MS63, $2500-$14,000) (PCGS MS64, $40,000 - $70,000), (PCGS MS65, $100,000)

Above is a 1936 double die cent.

There are three variations of this double die coin with degrees of doubling. DDO type one contains doubling in the date, LIBERTY, and the motto and considered the strongest shown in the photographs above. DDO type two shows doubling in the date. DDO 3 shows doubling in the motto and the date but it is not very pronounced.

1936 proof type II DDO (PCGS MS66, $5,400-$5,750)

1936 DDO 2 (PCGS MS65, $3500) (PCGS MS66, $11,500-$21,850)

1936 DDO 3 (PCGS MS65, $1700)

Small S   Large S

Above are photographs of the 1941 Large and small S.
There is no significant value between the two, only an interesting difference in dies used to mint the coins.

Above is the doubling for a 1941 Lincoln cent.
There are two degrees of doubling type I and type II. Double die I is in the motto and LIBERTY. The type II doubling confined to the motto and the four in the date.

Above is a 1941 full view double Motto and Liberty cent

Above is a photograph of a 1942-S over S Lincoln Cent.
There is also a triple S version of this coin.
1942-S S over S (ANACS EF45, $77) (NGC MS66, $287.50)
1942-S triple S (NGC MS65, $345) (NGC MS67, $432)

Above is a 1943-D D over D
Although not superior in the doubling of the D, this coin does command a premium in mint state conditions.
1942-D D over D (PCGS MS65, $300) 2015

Above is a PCGS sample of a 1943-S double die
From the photograph above the nine has apparent doubling. Some of the letters in LIBERTY show slight doubling.
1943-S DDO (PCGS MS67, 2325) 2015

Photograph above is a 1944 D over S issue.
1944 D over S (PCGS MS66, $2,200- $16,100) (PCGS MS65, $5,100-$5,462.50)

The photograph above is a PCGS 1951-D over D Lincoln cent.
The best method of detecting this hub/die error is to review the five in the date clearly deformed with extra metal. The D over D is much less apparent but doubled slightly.
1951-D over D (ANACS AU58, $12) 2014
1951-D over S (PCGS, MS66, $230-$300), NGC MS67, $2350) 2014

112

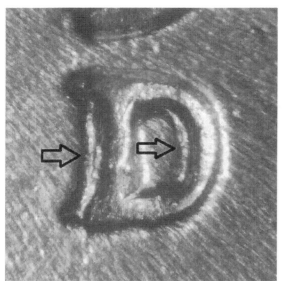

Above is a depiction of the D over D in the 1953-D Lincoln cent.
1953 D over D (PCGS MS65, $79) 2014

Above is a PCGS 1954 D/D/D mint error

The photograph above reveals a DDD triple error for the 1954 Lincoln cent. For the novice the appearance of this error does not provide a clear depiction of a triple D.

1954 D/D/D (ANACS MS65, $130) 2014

1955 Double die

One of the most sought after double die cents is the 1955. This coin was one of the first Lincoln cents to stir up collectors into seeking this coin. Most of these coins are in AU or mint state condition and this error coin quickly left circulation. The values of this coin range from $2000 to $10,000 for various grades in mint state condition. This coin is the most extreme of all doubled die mintages. Coin collecting in the 1950's was skyrocketing with the public and a passion for collecting was born.

1955 Double Die Lincoln cent

A 1955-D double die cent

114

The 1955-D double die shows a doubling of the one and the nine in the date. This coin does not command a large premium but it is a collectable error.

1955-D DDO (ANACS MS64, $42)

Pictured above is a 1955 S/S/S

This is a perfect triple S coin. Note how distinct the three S's are.

1955-S triple S RPM (PCGS MS64, $32-$92) RPM (ANACS MS65, $127) RPM (NGC MS66, $60)

Above is a 1956 D over D Lincoln Cent.

There are some variations of this coin error. The photographed picture above shows another D mintmark south of the normal D. In other 1956-D over D cents the D is directly or nearly over the normal D. This coin seems to come at a reasonable price at auction.

1956-D over D (ANACS AU58, $31) 2014

Pictured above is a PCGS 1956 DDS cent

This photograph reveals that there is a missed stamping but it is not entirely clear to see the D, D, S striking. Since the coin is a PCGS example, no questions for the experts.

1956 D/D/S (ANACS MS64, $40) 2014

A 1958 double die Lincoln cent

The coin has very strong doubling in the motto and LIBERTY.

Above is a 1960 D over D – approximate value is $800

117

Above is a photograph of a 1961 D over horizontal VI

1963-D Double die obverse. Strongest in the Motto – Value $25

!966 DDO – primarily in LIBERTY. Considered as a minor DDO

Above is a 1969-S double die cent. This coin can sell in excess of $50,000 in AU or better condition.

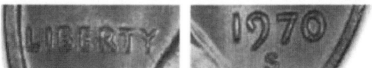

Above is a 1970-S double die large date with strong doubling in LIBERTY and motto– Value is approximately $540

Above is a 1971 DDO – doubled LIBERTY

1971-S DDO. Value in mint state ranges from $250-$500.

Above is an example of a 1972 double die – Value can exceed $7,000

Very rare 1974 Aluminum Lincoln cent. Only one known to exist.

1980 DDO. Strong doubling in LIBERTY –value exceeds $1500 in MS65 or better.

Above is a 1983 double die reverse, which can sell for over $1700.

1984 DDO Doubled ear and double beard

123

Photographs above show doubling for the 1995-D Lincoln cent.

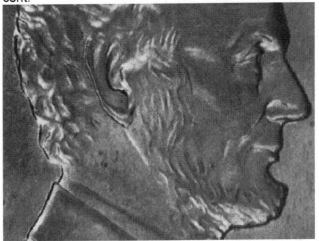

1997 double ear – This error can sell for $150 or more in MS65.

2006 DDO doubling in LIBERTY minor   PCGS MS65 $50

2014 DDO doubling in LIBERTY is minor. Value $150 MS64

BIE errors

Above is a "BIE" cent

A common error occurred with the Lincoln cents, especially in the 1950's. There is a distinct amount of extra material between the B and the E thus the notation of "BIE". There are full BIE coins such as the one shown above and partial BIE coins. The value of a BIE coin is generally less than $5. A large amount of BIE coins can be located in the 1950's, especially 1951-D, 1954-S, 1955-D, 1955-S, 1956, 1957, and 1957-D. Later dated BIE common coins include 1960-D, 1994 and 1995

Above is a full 1955 BIE error

Above is a 1994 BIE Lincoln cent

Above is a 1995 partial BIE error

BIE errors are common and come in various types of fills between the B and the E in Liberty. The best BIE error is a full line as shown in the first photograph above. There are many types of BIE errors for each date of occurrence.
BIE errors need to be uncirculated to obtain any significant value.

Wide AM Lincoln Cents

Located in proof sets, the discovery of some 1990 Lincoln cents without the S. About 300 of these coins exist with values exceeding $4000.

Until 1992, the US Mint manufactured cents with the wide AM. All 1993 and after issues intended to have a close AM for circulation. All proof Lincoln Cents issued from 1993 to 2009 should have the AM of America separated from one another. However, some proof 1998 and 1999 examples with the letters AM of America close to each other or almost touching exist, which indicates a mint state die used in place of a proof die. Since 1993, there have been several dates with both the wide and close AM. A 1992 with a closed AM is extremely rare. In proof sets, both the wide and close AM occur in 1998 and 1999. There are circulating examples of wide AM coins dated 1998 and 1999 along with the 2000 wide and closed AM which is most common.

2000 wide AM

The most common of all wide verses close AM's is the 2000-S proof set coin. The wide AM sells under $10

1999-S Wide AM – close AM

The 1999 Lincoln cents minted with two variations. The wide AM and the close AM, differentiated by the AM touching letters and a space between the A and the M.

128

The close AM can command $60 or more in various proof state conditions. The close AM is common in circulation intended coins.

1998-S wide AM – close AM

The 1998-S wide and close AM appears in proof sets. The 1998 close AM mint state encapsulated coin can sell in excess of $500

1992 close AM Only about 10 known examples. Very rare

1992-D close AM

Extremely rare to date. One of these coins sold at Heritage Auctions in AU condition for $5,640. The first coin located sold at HA for over $20,000 in MS64 condition.

For collectors searching for these errors, it will not be an easy task since the valuable errors reside in proof sets except for the very rare 1992-D.

There are numerous examples of Lincoln cents escaping the copper plating process in the US Mint resulting in partial of fully zinc coins in circulation. A wide range of prices exists for these coins, some in excess of $100 and others sell for less than $30. The weight of a normal Lincoln-copper plated zinc cent is 2.5 grams. Any coin missing the plating should weigh slightly under 2.5 grams.

There is the ability to take a copper-coated cent and plate it to give it the appearance that it is missing the copper coating. Coins that are plated will gain some weight and will therefore exceed 2.5 grams.

Lincoln cents missing clad layer

Authenticated 1999-D missing copper layer

There have been examples found of 1983 Lincoln cents that have been minted on copper planchets. These coins weight around 3.11 grams, which is the intended weight of all copper cents dated before 1982 and some 1982 issues.

Above is an authentic photograph of a 1983 copper cent.
At auction, this coin will sell in excess of $16,000.

Jefferson Nickel DDR and DDO

Double die Jefferson nickels errors are not as frequent as Lincoln cents and the number of error dates are lower.

Above is an example of a 1938 D over D Jefferson nickel. Value is approximately $100 in MS65 condition.

Above is an example of a 1939 double MONTICELLO. The MS67 example sold over in excess of $2300

1943 3 over 2 Jefferson nickel
Prices for this coin in mint state can exceed $2500

Above is the 1949-D over S Jefferson nickel. This coin can
command thousands in mint sate conditions. Mint state
$8000

Above is a 1953 DDO . The doubling on this coin is not extremely pronounced. The motto is most apparent. $90 mint state.

Roosevelt Dime DDR and DDO

Below are a few double die Roosevelt dimes to give the collector an idea of how to spot double dies in this series.

Mercury dime 1940-S double die date. Value $50-250 depending on the condition of the coin.

Mercury dime 2 over 1 – Wide range of values depending on the condition of the coin.

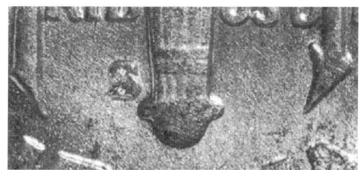

!948-S over S Roosevelt Dime - $25-$50 in mint state conditions.

1968-S Double S mint state $50

1968-S Double die reverse mint state $25

135

1968 Roosevelt dime no S
Some mint sets contained 1968 Roosevelt dimes with no S. Only
12 known to exist with a value of $12,000 or more.

1975-no S
The 1975 no S Roosevelt dime can be located in proof sets.
Only two known to exist selling in excess of $375,00

The mint used the 1968 proof reverse die to mint coins for circulation in 1968, 1969, and 1970. Below is the photographs of the two die reverses. The most noticeable difference is in the lines in the torch with deeply grooved lines in the proof die.

Normal reverse of a Roosevelt dime for circulation

Proof reverse of 1968

Washington quarter errors

1965 DDO Washington quarter – mint state $575
The 1965 double die Washington quarter show doubling in "IN GOD WE TRUST" and other lettering around the coin.

1967 SMS[26] DDO Washington quarter – minor doubling in LIBERTY-$150 in mint state.

---

[26] SMS - Special mint set

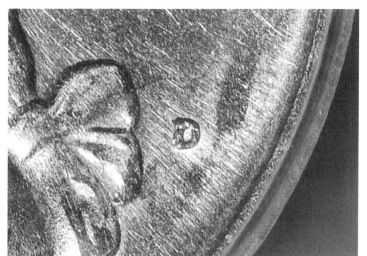

Above is a 1969-D over D double die. Value depending on grade $25-$50.

1776-1976 Washington quarter DDO - minor doubling in LIBERTY. PCGS AU58 $690

1990-S with strong doubling in the words IN GOD WE TRUST.

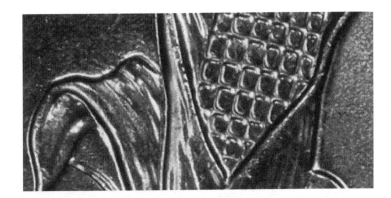

2004-D Extra Leaf high shown just below the larger leaf on the left.

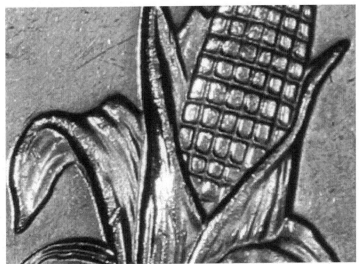

2004-D Extra left low shown just below the larger leaf on the left.
Both coins above can yield $150 or more in mint state conditions.

Half Dollar Double Dies and Oddities

Above is the 1946 double die half dollar mint state value $7000

Above is a 1955 Bugs Bunny Half
The lips of Franklin contain several lines.
Value approximately $200 in mint sate

141

1965 DDR with doubling primarily in the word UNITED.

Above is a 1966 Kennedy Half Double die -mint state $25

1967 DDR doubling pronounced in UNITED – Value mint
state $25

1971 DDO Kennedy half doubling in WE TRUST Value $100
in mint state conditions

1973-D Kennedy Half DDO. Minor doubling in LIBERTY-
Value MS65-$200

1974-D DDO Kennedy half. Primarily in WE TRUST. Value
$45-150 mint state conditions.

1776-1976 proof half DDR (PCGS MS65, $500)

144

1977-D Kennedy half minor doubling in IN GOD WE TRUST.
PCGS MS65 $650

Dollar errors

A truly rare and unique dollar with no S. Only one coin known to exist.

Amazing 2000 W dollar coin minted with 22 K gold. Only 39 of these minted. Twenty-seven melted by the mint and the remaining 12 were sent into space on the space shuttle Columbia and upon return were sent to Fort Knox.

The 2000 Dollar placed into boxes of Cheerios. Mintage occurred on 22 KT gold in error. Coin values range from $4000 - $6000.

References:
- The Official American Numismatic Association Grading Standards for United States Coins" edited by Kenneth Bressett.
- The US Mint site – www.usmint.org
- The Lincoln cent resource – www.lincolncentresource.com

Glossary

ANA – American Numismatic Association. The ANA provides insights to coin collecting. Anyone can join ANA for a small fee.

Blank – A raw planchet that is ready for striking.

Clipped Planchet – A raw blank missing part of the circumference or other portion of the coin is a clipped planchet.

Cud – A die break usually found around the circumference of the coin.

Denomination – The face value of a coin or bill. The Lincoln cent denomination is one cent.

Die – A die is a punch that contains a face of the design used to imprint on a planchet.

Die crack – A raised line appears on the surface of a coin as the metal fills in where the die has cracked.

Die Errors - Die errors caused by the mint dies wearing down over time or dies that have not been prepared identical to others.

DDO – The designation for coins that contain a double die obverse

DDR – The designation for coins that contain a double die reverse.

DMM – double mint- mark

Double Die – A distinct doubling of the lettering and or the date on a coin created from the dies.

eBay – An auction site designed for people to buy and sell various items.

Flow lines – There are lines shown of the surface of the coin caused by the spreading of the metal in striking.

Heritage Auctions – A company that sells items on line and through live auctions.

Hub – The punch used to create the dies used to press the design on a coin. The design is opposite of the actual die image.

Mint Mark – The mint places a letter on most coins to represent the site of mintage.

D – Denver

S – San Francisco

P – Philadelphia (also no min- mark)

W – West Point

CC – Carson City

O – New Orleans

Mint Striking Errors - Collectors and organizations dedicated to collecting coins regard mint striking errors as those created by the minting process. Most of these coins command no significant value, especially those that have no date. DDO – A coin with doubling on the obverse relates double die obverse.

DDR – A coin with doubling on the reverse - a double die reverse.

MPD –A date or multiple dates appear in different places on the coin.

Mule – A coin that minted on the incorrect planchet is a mule.

Numismatist – A person that studies and accumulates knowledge of coins is a numismatist.

Obverse – The front of a coin

Off center – A coin that struck outside of the collar that holds the coin in place for minting.

OMM – Over mint- mark – coins that are stuck with one mint mark and then a different mint mark.

Over dates – One date on the coin is over or under another date.

Planchet – The blank annealed that to make a coin

Planchet Error – A coin minted with a defective blank considered a planchet error.

RPM – Re-punched mint mark. The mint takes dies that are of one mint- mark and re-punches the die with another mint-mark. Traces of the original mint- mark remain creating an error coin.

Sandwich Coin – The interior of a coin is one alloy covered by another alloy on both sides. Modern day silver coins contain copper interiors with silver plating on both sides.

Variations - Variations are not mint errors in the technical sense. Variations in coins caused by creating hubs and dies that are not exactly the same resulting in dates that can be compared as large to small, wide to thin etc.

Whizzing – The process of using high-pressure water and brushes to clean the surface of a coin noted as whizzing. Whizzing significantly reduces the value of a coin.

We want to answer all questions pertaining to coins or the content of this guide. Please feel free to email us at: McDonald.Stan@comcast.net

Made in the USA
Lexington, KY
16 February 2017